ASTROLOGICAL

KEYS

to

Self-actualization

&

Self-realization

ASTROLOGICAL

KEYS

to

Self-actualization

&

Self-realization

CLARA A. WEISS

SAMUEL WEISER
New York

First published in 1980
Samuel Weiser, Inc.
740 Broadway
New York, N.Y. 10003

ISBN 0-87728-509-8

Typesetting and layout by
Positive Type
Millerton, N.Y.

Printed in the U.S.A. by
Noble Offset Printers, Inc.
New York, N.Y. 10003

Contents

Introduction, 1
Definitions, 8
Aries, 13
Taurus, 21
Gemini, 29
Cancer, 37
Leo, 45
Virgo, 53
Libra, 60
Scorpio, 67
Sagittarius, 74
Capricorn, 80
Aquarius, 88
Pisces, 95
Polarity, 103
Wholeness, 110
Bibliography, 113

The writer wishes to express grateful acknowledgment to all those who have aided in the development of this booklet. Particular thanks go to Joel Zavies for his work on the manuscript.

INTRODUCTION

In offering astrological keys to Self-Actualization and Self-Realization, our task is of a general nature, not a specific one. Our purpose is to present some of the salient features in each zodiacal sign which combine to form a synthetic influence affecting a growth in consciousness of the personality and an increasing identification with the Soul, the Higher or Transpersonal Self.

Our aim is to give merely a guideline, a primer of special astrological information that may assist in furthering Self-Actualization and Self-Realization, serving as an addition to the methods now being used in developing these processes. We feel that these complementary activities conditioning the "whole" man can be aided in widening their perspective through the knowledge of certain astrological factors which have been and continue to be contributory influences in man's evolutionary progress.

Through recognition of particular cosmic energies and forces that are registering a subtle effect on his nature, an individual can become better equipped to handle them and thus assume more control in integrating the component parts of his personality as well as gain a greater awareness of his personality and inner Self, that synthesizing Center, the informing life, the very essence of his Being.

We realize that in just highlighting some outstanding aspects of the zodiacal signs, we reduce this manual to a very abbreviated outline which will only suggest the picture of the "whole" man. However, this may be supplemented by a detailed horoscope mathematically calculated which can provide an accurate blueprint of his potentials.

• • •

The interpretation given in this handbook is based mainly on the teachings of the Eastern sage, the Master Djwhal Khul, as given to Alice A. Bailey in many of her numerous writings on esotericism.

Foremost in consideration are the concepts set forth in her book, *Esoteric Astrology*, where she defines the occult approach to astrology marking the distinction of interpretation between exoteric and esoteric astrology as presented in the Ageless Wisdom. She says:

> Exoteric astrology deals with the characteristics and qualities of the personality and of the form aspects, and also with events, happenings, circumstances, and the conditioning environment which appear in the personal horoscope, indicative of planetary control and not of solar control. Esoteric astrology concerns itself primarily with the unfoldment of consciousness, with the impacts which awaken it to the peculiar "gifts" of any particular sign and ray (cosmic energy) endowment and with the reaction of the man and his consequent enrichment through his response to the influence of a sign, working through the esoteric* planets from the angle of humanitarian awareness, of discipleship,* and of initiation.**

Since the point of view set forth in *Esoteric Astrology* is uncommon, we thought it would be helpful to know something of the purpose that the Master Djwhal Khul had for presenting this particular aspect of esoteric teaching. The following excerpts give an abbreviated idea of this which is more fully explained in *A Treatise on the Seven Rays* (Esoteric Astrology, Volume III):

---

*See section entitled, "Definitions."
**Esoteric Astrology, A Treatise on the Seven Rays, Vol. III, pp. 145-146.

I seek to lay the ground for a somewhat new approach—a far more esoteric approach—to the science of astrology. Certain things I may say will probably be regarded by the academic and uninspired astrologer as revolutionary, or as erroneous, as improbable or unprovable...I would ask all of you who read (Esoteric Astrology) to preserve a willingness to consider hypotheses and to make an effort to weigh a theory or suggestion and to test out the conclusions over the course of a few years...

I shall not...deal with the subject of esoteric astrology from the standpoint of the horoscope at all...(But the emphasis is on)...universal relationships, the interplay of energies, the nature of what lies behind the Great Illusion, the deluding 'Appearances of things as they are' and the destiny of our planet, of the kingdoms in nature and of humanity as a whole—these will constitute the major part of our theme.

I will indicate, if I can, the subjective realities of which the outer illusion is but the phenomenal appearance, conditioned by men's thoughts throughout the ages; I will emphasize the fact of *the livingness* of the Sources from which all energies and forces which play upon our planet flow and emanate; I will endeavour, above all else, to demonstrate to you, that all-pervading unity and that underlying synthesis which is the basis of all religions and of all the many transmitted forces...to show you how you are a part of a greater whole of which you can become consciously aware when you can function as souls, but of which you are today unconscious, or at least only registering and sensing the inner reality in which you live and move and have your being...

...Astrology is *essentially* the purest presentation of occult truth in the world at this time, because it is the science which deals with those conditioning and governing energies and forces which play through and upon the whole world of space and all that is found within that field...

The Tibetan Teacher, as the Master DK is often called, feels that when this fact is more fully understood, relationships between individual, planetary, systemic and cosmic entities will be more truly evaluated and then 'we shall begin to live scientifically which is the immediate purpose of astrology to bring about.'

The method used in his teaching is to work from the universal to the particular and from the general to the specific but to be clearly understood that the emphasis is on the universal and the general and not on the particular and the specific for the application of truth to the specific lies in the hands of students of astrology.

A point to be kept in mind relates to the twelve constellations of the zodiac: they are constantly receiving energies from varied sources which become blended and fused with the energy of a particular constellation where they are transmuted and "occultly refined" before eventually reaching our solar system. Something that we are apt to overlook is the influence of our own globe, the Earth. Its radiation comes direct to us from the planet itself and since we are in the midst of it we tend to forget its power.

● ● ●

Undoubtedly there will be those who will wonder why certain aspects of the teaching have been omitted in this handbook. The reason is that in selecting material for a booklet, simplification and brevity demanded delineations of such influential factors as the Decanates, the Crosses, the Triangles et al for an abbreviated text. Full description of the part they play can be found in *A Treatise on the Seven Rays* (Esoteric Astrology, Volume III).

However, an exception is made for those who have their own horoscopes or intend to have a chart made. Although the Tibetan does not deal with these calculations he offers an interpretation of the *Sun Sign* and the *Ascendant* which, in throwing new light on them, may increase or widen one's perspective.

The Sun Sign, according to the Ageless Wisdom, "indicates the *present* problem of the man; it sets the pace or established tempo of his personality life; it is related to quality, to temperament and the life tendencies which are seeking expression during this particular incarnation, and it is suggestive of the rajasic or the activity aspect of the innate man. Fundamentally, the forces here found are indicative of the line of least resistance.

"It refers to the nature of the man, physical, mental and spiritual. It holds the secret of the personality ray (energy) and of the man's responsiveness, or lack of responsiveness, to the Soul, the real man. It indicates also the integration already achieved (Self-Actualization, Ed.) and the present point of unfoldment of the soul qualities, of the present available equipment, of the present life quality and of the immediately possible group relations. It relates, from the angle of the Ageless Wisdom, nothing more."*

The Ascendant or rising sign "indicates the intended life or immediate soul purpose for this incarnation. It holds the secret of *the future* (Self-Realization, Ed.) and presents the force which rightly used will lead the man to success. It represents the satvic or harmony aspect of life and can produce right relationship between soul and personality in any one incarnation. It thus points the way to the recognition of the force of the soul."*

Dane Rudhyar adds to the picture:

> In every human individual...the characteristic qualities of each of the twelve zodiacal signs operate in varying degrees. However, one, or a very few, of these qualities... predominate. It is such a predominance which determines the type to which the individual belongs—his dominant zodiacal type...**

More and more today the idea of the "whole" man is seeping into the public consciousness. What may seem new, or fairly new, to the West has long permeated the thinking of the East. We hear it described by Elmer Green as he presents a particular concept:

> The destiny of the individual man is to develop aware-ness *in* and then to integrate all levels of his nature into one Being, a being who is a man of earth and at the same time has correct moral development and super-conscious aware-ness.***

*Drawn from *Esoteric Astrology* pp. 3-19.
***Triptych*, "Gifts of the Spirit," pp. 18, 19.
***From the Menninger Foundation paper given at the Conference on Voluntary Control of Internal States, Council Grove, Kansas; April 17, 1969. p. 7.

Self-Actualization and Self-Realization are concerned with the "whole" man. For the layman, the term, "Self-Actualization" is more easily understood than its complement, "Self-Realization," for the former relates to the "I" consciousness regarded as "an awakening or manifestation of man's potentials expressed in several fields including the ethical, the aesthetic, the religious, and others."

On the other hand, Self-Realization is apt to be nebulous and vague in a man's thinking, for it refers to a happening not often experienced, a very high state of awareness of almost infinite variety, as each individual reaches it according to a particular response. Those acquainted with the analysis given of the "peak experience" by Abraham Maslow gain some idea of what occurs when contact with the Higher Self is realized:

> The "peak experience" seems to lift us to greater than normal heights so that we see and perceive in a higher than usual way. We become larger, greater, stronger, bigger, taller people and tend to perceive accordingly.
>
> In peak experiences...dichotomies, polarities and conflicts of life tend to be transcended or resolved. That is to say, there tends to be a moving towards the perception of unity and integration in the world. The person himself tends to move towards fusion, integration and unity and away from splitting conflict and oppositions...The person feels himself the creative center of his own perceptions—more self-determined, more a free agent with more "free will"...than at any other time...more of a person, more subject to the laws of gratitude or all-embracing love for everybody and for everything, leading to an impulse to do something good for the world...even a sense of obligation and dedication.
>
> The peak experience is felt as a self-validating, self-justifying moment which carries its own intrinsic value with it... It is felt to be a highly valuable—even uniquely valuable—experience, so great an experience sometimes that even to attempt to justify it takes away from its dignity and worth.*

*Religions, Values and Peak-Experiences, p. 61, 62, 65, 67, 68.

In order to relate this activity to astrological happenings our endeavor is to show how the Zodiacal Signs, the Rays and the Planetary Rulers of the signs contribute to the picture by the influence of *their* qualities. Experience in each of the twelve celestial areas can be thought of as an adventure in growth and elevation where the expanding consciousness gradually leads to a synthesis expressing the "whole" man.

DEFINITIONS

When terms used in a text have a specific meaning which are not familar to the reader, frustration in understanding easily arises. And so to avoid this the following interpretations are offered for clarification.

Esoteric. That which lies hidden below the surface of ordinary meaning or knowledge or general reference.

Self-Actualization. The integration of the personality, the lower self, with its three vehicles of expression—the physical, emotional and mental bodies.

Self-Realization. Identification with the Higher Self, the Soul, the Transpersonal Self.

Soul. The result of the union of Father-Spirit and Mother-Matter, the mediating principle between the two. It is that which lies at the center of every form, be it an atom or a star; in a human being it manifests as consciousness. As an integral part of the Universal Soul it can become aware of the Purpose of Deity and can intelligently cooperate with the Will of God and work with the Plan of Evolution.

Spiritual. The word relates to attitudes and relationships on every level of the cosmic physical plane—from the lowest to the highest....The word "Spiritual" refers to every effect of the evolutionary process as it drives man forward from one range of sensitivity and of responsiveness to impression to another; it relates to the expansion of consciousness, so that the unfoldment of the organs of sensory impression in primitive man or in the awakening infant are just as surely spiritual events as participation in an initiatory process; the development of the so-called irreligious man into a sound and effective businessman, with all the necessary perception and equipment for success, is as much a spiritual unfoldment—in that individual's experience—as the taking of an initiation by a disciple in an Ashram.

...."spiritual" relates...to the moving forward from one level of consciousness (no matter how low or gross from the view of a higher level of contact) to the next; it is related to the power to see the vision, even if that vision is materialistic as seen from the angle of a higher registration of possibility...

...all activity which drives the human being forward towards some form of development (physical, emotional, intuitional and so forth) is essentially spiritual in nature and is indicative of the livingness of the inner divine entity.

...The discoveries of science...or the production of some great work in literature or in the field of art, are just as much an evidence of 'spiritual' unfoldment as the rhapsodies of the mystic or the registration by the so-called occultist of a contact with the Hierarchy (the Spiritual Guides of Humanity).*

Signs of the Zodiac. In the teaching of the Ageless Wisdom, the signs serve a dual purpose in affecting man's spiritual growth according to his point in evolution, i.e., one, his *descent* into *matter* (life in form), two, his *ascent* out of it into the realm of *spirit.* More detailed information is given in the description of each individual sign. The dates given for the signs are approximate.

Planetary Ruler. When a planet has a rapport with a sign and is in close relationship with it, the planet is considered to be its "ruler" and acts as a carrier for the characteristic qualities of its energies.

---

*The Rays and the Initiations, A Treatise on the Seven Rays, Vol. V, pp. 3644-5.

Vulcan. According to the Ageless Wisdom this planet is among the approximately 70 "hidden" ones yet to be discovered. The energy of Vulcan carrying the First Ray of Will and Power, with the will-to-be, stimulates both selfishness and unselfishness. It supplies the capacity to endure, to persist with continuity of effort. Its force influences only those who have achieved certain spiritual growth.

Cosmic Rays. These are streams of energies originating in the seven stars of the Great Boar—Ursa Major. The word "ray" is merely a name for a certain type of energy. Although these great forces (seven in number) create all forms, they do not emphasize the structures themselves but the qualities that the forms radiate, and in so doing become a means to express Divine Purpose.

Logos. The informing life which lies at the center of a cosmic, solar or planetary system. *The earth's Logos is the Planetary Spirit*—the One in Whom we live and move and have our being. He is represented and expressed by Sanat Kumara, a Great Being, who presides over the Great Council at Shamballa where the Will of God is known. The Logos is God Transcendant, and in form, God Immanent.

The Plan. This is as much of Divine Purpose as can be brought into expression upon the planet under the Law of Evolution at any one time or particular epoch in time and space. One of its aims is to produce subjective synthesis in humanity. It will also produce in man an intelligent cooperation with the Divine Purpose. In relation to Self-(Soul) Realization, it emphasizes growth of the Group idea, of the Group good, Group understanding, Group interrelations and Group goodwill—revealing to humanity true and inner synthesis, a realization of the unity of all beings and the unity of divine objective. The Plan has three great goals: the revelation of love, the illumination of the mind and the evocation of the Will.

The Hierarchy. The spiritual Hierarchy of the Planet, the Elder Brothers of Humanity who have triumphed over matter, mastered all experiences on the physical plane and, having passed beyond human evolution, have attained a very advanced stage of spiritual development. They are characterized by an enduring love, always acting for the good of the group. They are in charge of The Plan and where humanity is concerned, work with the spiritual nature of the Soul. Referred to as the Masters of the Wisdom and the Lords of Compassion, They dwell in a dimension above the human kingdom called the Kingdom of Souls—the Fifth Kingdom.

The Twelve Creative Hierarchies. A group of energies, *outside the solar system,* whose interlocking rays play through and stimulate every part of it. Latent germs of force centers, they exist as the aggregate of germ lives, giving impulse, providing the model and procuring through their existence the raison d'etre of all that is seen on all planes. They manifest subjectively and flower forth and express themselves through the medium of a form or group of forms. Gathered upon the sum total of these vital bodies is the dense material which we regard as evolutionary matter and thus becomes the foundation for it. Sometimes these cosmic forces which operate far beyond our solar system express themselves through another hierarchy such as humanity; hence humanity is known as the Fourth Creative Hierarchy but is not the Hierarchy itself.

The subject is far too abstruse to be discussed in this primer. It can be explored more fully in *Esoteric Astrology* where it is explained in detail. However, since these cosmic influences are part of the over-all astrological pattern, they need to be included in the picture of each sign.

Ashram. A meeting place of minds where members of a Master's group seek to forward the expression of the Evolutionary Plan on earth to the degree of their understanding of its pattern and program.

Glamour. A form of illusion occuring on the astral or emotional plane which distorts Reality with many aspects of apparent Truth.

The Ageless Wisdom, The Ancient Wisdom, The Wisdom Teaching. ...a vast body of information that has existed since prehistoric time and which deals with the constitution and evolution both of man and of the whole universe. Knowledge of the Teaching can act as a means to evaluate the wholeness of life and the trend of evolution.

"The Ageless Wisdom is based upon the realization that the world is created upon a system of exact vibration, patterns, symbols and dimensions; and through studying them in depth one is able to gain some understanding of the purpose and progression of the created world and the Great Consciousness behind it."*

Disciple. One who is pledged to serve his fellow men and is aware of his lower nature. Realizing that his weaknesses are hindrances to achieving spiritual unfoldment, he proceeds to surmount them and fulfill his spiritual destiny through the unfoldment of his personality and identification with the Soul. And in so doing he attempts to serve humanity and the Hierarchy in implementing the Plan.

Initiation. Experience in spiritual growth, a progressive entry into higher levels of consciouness which has to do with "the conscious development of the self (the personality) and the wisdom aspect of the One Self (the soul)."* "...an initiation is in reality a crisis, a climaxing event, and is only truly brought about when the disciple has learnt patience, endurance and sagacity in emerging from the many preceding and less important crises...a culminating episode made possible because of the self-inspired discipline in which the disciple has forced himself to conform."**

"Man...grows through expansions of self-conscious realisations, self-initiated and self-imposed. It is the line of aspiration and of conscious endeavour, and is the most difficult line of development in the solar system, for it follows not along the line of least resistance, but seeks to initiate and impose a higher rhythm."*

There are nine initiations—I, Birth; II, Baptism; III, Transfiguration; IV, Renunciation; V, Revelation; VI, Decision; VII, Resurrection; VIII, Transition; IX, Refusal. The first two initiations are considered as those of the threshold, the third as the first major one.**

Initiation, Human and Solar p. 97
**The Rays and the Initiations* A Treatise on the Seven Rays Vol. V, pp. 662, 685-687

ARIES, THE RAM
March 21 - April 20

Testing, trial, desire, illumination, form and salvation are among the keynotes of our solar system and the spiritual adventure of knowing them begins in Aries.

Aries is the first sign of the zodiac where the cycle of manifestation starts. The Soul, in response to the highest aspect of Deity, is awakened to take form with the *will-to-incarnate:*

> to reach the lowest and there control, to know the uttermost and thus face all experience.

Beginning-Creation-Evolution are the signposts of activity in this sign of the Ram.

Beginning has endless meanings in its wide latitude of reference, be it some human project or cosmic action "that reveals the life of God swinging into action as it forms the birthplace of some universal idea—God in manifestation."*

Creation for the Soul begins with the drawing unto itself, for the first time, its initial vehicles of expression in form—its mental body in Aries, its desire body in the following sign of Taurus, and its etheric or vital sheath in Gemini; all to be used subjectively. But not until the fourth sign—Cancer—is reached does the Soul appropriate a dense physical vehicle that the eye can recognize.

Esoteric Astrology, A Treatise on the Seven Rays, Vol. III, p. 92.

Four words mark the changes in progressive evolutionary development:

1. *Re-creation* produces the pull into incarnation on the physical plane. This is accomplished by the combined influence of Cancer and Aries;

2. *Re-generation* creates those interior changes which eventually lead to:

3. *Re-orientation,* the cycle of repolarization when the personality recedes into the background;

4. *Renunciation* is the final stage when the initiate renounces all for the love of humanity and its service and lays himself upon the altar of sacifice and, as a result, the final liberation.*

The various energies which play upon the human being and produce his unfoldment constitute his field of experience. Those two words—unfoldment and experience—should never be linked, for each produces the other. As one is subjected to experience in the field of the form world, a paralleling unfoldment of consciousness is carried forward. As that unfoldment produces constant changes in realization and a consequent reorientation to a new state of awareness, it necessarily leads to new experience—experience of fresh phenomena, of new states of being, and of dimensional conditions hitherto unknown.**

The keynotes that show the Arian objectives all convey the same idea symbolically:

1. To express the will-to-be and do.
2. To unfold the power to manifest.
3. To enter into battle for the Lord.
4. To arrive at unity through effort.***

Long and arduous testing confronts the man on his evolutionary journey before he is able to achieve his goal. In the beginning and for an inordinate time the personality is in control and desire of the senses are gratified. But eventually, satiety

---

*Esoteric Astrology, A Treatise on the Seven Rays, Vol. III, p. 107.
**A Treatise on White Magic, p. 374.
***Esoteric Astrology, p. 93.

supplants this satisfaction and the "seeker" begins to realize that if he is to find fulfillment of a persistent *longing*, he will have to search elsewhere to satisfy his need. This he does by directing his search inward. When this happens, the attention of the Soul is caught. Up to this point the Higher Self has taken no interest in its instrument for expression. But now it begins to throw its guiding light downward into its vehicle, and with this "fusion," the climb out of *Matter* starts.

● ● ●

Each of the zodiacal signs is associated with one of the four elements—fire, air, earth and water. Aries is a member of the fire triplicity which includes Leo and Sagittarius, each sign expressing a different aspect of fire.

Aries brings *electric fire* — Spirit
Leo, *solar fire* — Soul
Sagittarius, *fire by friction* — Body

Fire can nourish with heat or destroy with flame. *Ignis Sanat* purifies by cleansing and testifies to the interpretation of the biblical pronouncement, "Our God is a consuming fire" (Hebrews, 12:29). The fiery God acts as a purifying agent who clears away the dross that Love may prevail, for "God is Love."

Cosmic Rays and Planetary Rulers

THE RAYS

Of the Seven Rays controlling all forms of life, three make their influence felt in this sign of the Ram: the *Sixth Ray of Devotion and Idealism*, exoterically, the *Fourth Ray of Harmony through Conflict*, esoterically, and the *First Ray of Will or Power*, hierarchically.

The Sixth Ray of Devotion or Idealism, like all other energies, can influence either positively or negatively. On its constructive side this ray fosters vision of the ideal and devotion to it; on the negative side, it operates in an exaggerated intensity and becomes fanaticism. It has been pointed out that "by nature, man is devoted to whatever may be his goal in life, be it to raise a family, to acquire property or discipleship...Whatever it may be, he is devoted to it."

When this ray is casting its power esoterically, it embodies the principle of recognition—the capacity to see reality behind form, to distinguish it from appearance and because of this faculty it is able to recognize "causes." As an expression of *Will* it stimulates the desire to seek these causes, to discover ideas and the motive power behind them—to discover the working out of "the energising Principle, Life, Being; for the Will is the cause, hence *The Will to Causation.*"*

After a man has achieved a measure of personality integration and is beginning to establish a rhythm of contact with the Soul, he responds to the vibrations of this ray, sets his ideals on a high level, and strives to reach them.

The Fourth Ray of Harmony through Conflict is the "refiner," the producer of perfection within the form; it is the ray that governs humanity with the objective of harmonizing the higher and lower principles both in the individual and in the Whole.

Its activity involves conflict and struggle. The ensuing pain and struggle break up the limitations that hinder mental development. This phase of suffering often becomes the means to create artistic expression and the pain endured is tranmuted into beauty, illustrating cause and effect. Throughout all the experiences there is developed mental growth leading to spiritual unfoldment.

The Fourth Ray is the ray of the intuition and confers the power of higher perception which permits man to receive impressions from the cosmic Fourth Dense Physical Plane, the Buddhic. The "harmony" aspect of this ray is the goal to be achieved after all trials and tribulations have been overcome.

The First Ray of Will or Power is classified as a Ray of Aspect, one of the major rays including the Second and the Third. It is concerned with the Life aspect and the destruction of forms to pave the way for the building of new ones by the Second Ray. This *destroying* is in reality a positive aspect ordinarily not understood, particularly when the energy of the Will is being expressed dynamically as power. Persistence is a major characteristic of this energy and the production of ideas a constant activity.

Before the First Ray reaches our solar system to make its strong impact with the will-to-create and the will-to-destroy, it is

*Esoteric Astrology. p. 601.

focussed in Aries. Called the "Finger of God," it is truly beneficial for as it destroys, it produces detachment from form and the destruction of all that is standing in the way of ongoing spiritual unfoldment. An illustration of this is, "life in the seed which destroys successively all forms that fruition may eventuate." From this comes another First Ray title—"The Divine Incentive."

Always this First Ray of Will or Power supplies the impulse of promoting or forwarding the "new"; in reality, it fulfills the need for change in the patterns for growth—"No man putteth new wine into old bottles...new wine must be put into new bottles." (Luke, 5: 37-8.)

THE PLANETS

Mars, the exoteric ruler of Aries (a modification of Ares, the Greek name for the God of War), is the carrier for the Sixth Ray of Devotion and Idealism and is associated with battle, struggle, forcefulness and courage. When devotion becomes abnormal, fanaticism results. Mars can lead to both war and evolution.

Symbols, according to prophecy, will be the alphabet of the future. If one recalls the ancient Chinese proverb, "One picture is worth a thousand words," we see in the two down-turned horns of the ram—the astrological symbol of Aries—a suggestion of the battering power of the animal who fights head on, significant of the latent drive of those born when the earth is aligned with the sun at the beginning of spring.

God's idea in Aries under the impulse of Mars is finally concretized into a plan in Capricorn, whether the objective is the full flowering of planetary life in all forms or the working out of a personality idea perhaps some world project or the aspiration of an initiate whose worldly ambition is being transmuted into its highest aspect, seeking to develop God's plans and make them his own.

Mercury. This esoteric ruler has the familiar wings on his helmet and wings on his feet revealing him as the fleet messenger of the Gods whose primary activity is mediating. This mediating may be between Soul and personality, or between the higher and lower mind, between two souls or two minds. But *always the activity is mental,* expressing the quality of the Fourth Ray of Harmony through Conflict of which Mercury is the carrier-agent.

This influence, however, is not registered by the disciple until he has made the decision to follow the road of serving humanity.

Time and again this planet creates hurdles that have to be surmounted before growth in consciousness can move onward. This involves dissipating illusion by the Soul that throws its light into the lower mind to free it from the veils that hide the Truth.

Keywords sometimes used interchangeably with keynotes give the direction for progress on the path of evolutionary progress, downward or upward. When the life is self-centered and personality gain is the goal, the note rings out: *Let form be sought.* For the Soul the voice proclaims: *I come forth from the plane of mind, I rule.*

Uranus. God of the Sky and the Ether, this planet is the only one to channel the energy of the Seventh Ray whose purpose is to relate Spirit and Matter which it does by bringing together *electric fire and fire by friction.* In addition it strongly reflects an aspect of the First Ray of Will and Power, since Uranus is the planet of occultism and possesses great potency.

It has been said that when the Christ proclaimed, "I am Alpha and Omega," (Revelations, 1:18) he was associating the "beginning and the end" with the sign of Aries whose "impulsing" energy enabled Him to inaugurate the New Age in whose antechamber we now find ourselves. When an initiate has become a savior in Pisces and enters again in Aries, he then ascends on a turn of the spiral to new heights in the realm of the Higher Evolution and moves onward to participate in greater cosmic service.

Self-Actualization and Self-Realization

> A human being is not one thing among others; things determine each other, but *man* is ultimately self-determining. What he becomes—within the limits of endowment and environment—he has made out of himself.*

For the Arian, the first key to Self-Actualization is to hold in check his natural exuberance and enthusiasm (Mars) lest they deprive him of a sense of proportion. It is Mars that endows him

Man's Search for Meaning.

with the courage to do and dare and with fearlessness stand steady at the center of his being; to awaken those forces that lie behind the compulsive energy that make him a natural leader, a competent captain rather than a wise general.

Aries in relation to the physical body rules the head, and strong disciplined mental control of the emotions must be acquired to forge the personality into a receptive instrument capable of receiving impressions from the Higher Self. Identification with this Transpersonal Self makes it possible to receive intuitive perception which the Soul provides.

The Arian problems concern the ability to distinguish between the urges of the little self, (the promptings of the "I" consciousness) and the impressions of the true self, (the Soul). The demand is for readiness to forfeit gratification of desires, and the ability to sublimate them in striving to express the qualities of the Self; to serve and not demand true service, and never to impose rule over others but to wield power with love intelligently applied.

It is obvious that the combative energies, so strong in the Arian nature, evoke the need for transmutation and transformation which will allow the Transpersonal Self to direct all energy toward humanitarian goals. Although the average personality achieves only partial success in attempting to reach transcendence in the sign of the Ram, this endeavor awakens a realization that there is still a greater spiritual objective and thus there results an increase in consciousness which supplies valuable understanding.

Patience and perseverance must become the handmaidens for the Arian if he is to overcome his tendency to procrastinate, to start something but not finish it—an indication of early but unsustained enthusiasm. What he greatly needs is to become not the warrior who batters his way to outer success, but the "warrior within" who gains spiritual understanding, whose life intention is geared toward synthesis. His assets of hopefulness and enthusiasm must be handled wisely so as not to lead to recklessness and fanaticism—ever the extremes to be avoided. Very much later in his evolutionary progress, his qualities will be balanced by those of his polar opposite, Libra.

> Truth is within ourselves; it takes no rise
> From outward things; whate'er you may believe.

There is an inner centre in us all,
Where Truth abides in fullness; and around
Wall upon wall, the gross flesh hems it in,
This perfect, clear perception—which is Truth.
A baffling and perverted carnal flesh
Binds it, and makes all error; and to *know*
Rather consists in opening out a way
Whence the imprisoned splendour may escape,
Than in affecting entry for a light
Supposed to be without.

Paracelsus, Robert Browning

When Self-Actualization has reached the point where inclusiveness prevails as an attitude, where the right kind of devotion manifests a poise and stillness reflecting identification with the Inner Being—"Be still and hear God"—then the vision of the true goal is revealed, and the man treading the path of helping his fellow men becomes at-one with the reflection of Spirit—the Soul.

TAURUS, THE BULL
April 21 - May 21

Man is a being in search of meaning. —Plato

Learning is not the accumulation of scraps of knowledge. It is a *growth*, where every act of knowledge develops the learner, thus making him capable of constituting ever more and more complex objectivities—and the object growth in complexity parallels the subjective growth in capacity.*

The Bull of God—His Majesty, Taurus—so often is pictured with a single eye in his forehead from which radiate lines of light symbolizing the goal of this second sign of the zodiac—*Illumination.*

The light of the body is the eye; if therefore, thine eye be single, thy whole body shall be full of light.
—Matthew 6:22

Because Taurus symbolizes Desire in all its phases, it is known as the sign of the major life incentive. Its activity is struggle whether it is individual, group, planetary or cosmic. Its basic

Love and Will, page 223.

quality demonstrates as desire in the mass of men, stubborness in the average man; an adherance to personality aims or as will intelligently expressed, activated by the impulse of love in the advanced man.

Illumination eventually emerges out of the struggle of the two halves of a whole, material desire and spiritual will. Desire-Will is said to underlie all forms on all levels and exhibits the force of the form-nature while Will, the energy of the Soul, manifests as direction and conformity to the Plan. This Plan has many interpretations; one of its simplest definitions is that it is as much as the individual man can sense of its pattern according to his point in evolution.

The process of spiritual unfoldment is exceedingly slow and commences only after some measure of personality integration has been achieved. Before this stage has been reached the personality has not shown sufficient sensitivity to awaken the interest of the Soul. But when the personality bodies have become coordinated to act as a unit, the higher self, sensing a quality of receptiveness in its instrument, starts to pour light into the lower self and fusion begins to be generated.

All signs are characterized by one of the four elements of fire, air, earth and water. Taurus is an earth sign, part of the triplicity including Virgo and Capricorn. Because of the earthiness of his nature, the Taurean must conquer his weaknesses on the physical level for it is only on this plane that the living experience can activate growth. When this happens desire becomes transmuted into aspiration. Aspiration then becomes some expression of the Will of God which has to be stepped down to become the Will-to-Good, and is later expressed as Goodwill. During this long period of transition, the Soul plays a dual role. Not only does it affect changes in the form but Soul-light produces sequentially the revelation of it and in Taurus it is the "penetrating light of the Path."*

Gautama, the Buddha, is closely connected with the sign of the Bull. It seems something more than coincidence that his birth, illumination and death all occurred at the time of the full moon of Taurus. The right control of desire so basic in Buddha's teaching is likewise a major problem for the striving Taurean disciple.

*Esoteric Astrology, p. 329.

Suffering and pain in some form invariably accompany the struggle for growth. For the man seeking enlightenment it is of great help to appreciate that these trials and tribulations are in reality beneficent challenges providing crucibles to distill his potentials. They act as future tests for the "burning ground" and the "battle ground," ordeals by fire, which in true perspective are recognized as "the light of knowledge being released within the field of wisdom."

Cosmic Rays and Planetary Rulers

THE RAYS

All rays are considered to be the expression of Great Beings— a concept to be taken hypothetically if not accepted as a reality.

The Fifth Ray of Concrete Mind or Science. This energy reveals the quality of a Divine Being who is interpreting Divine Will on a lower plane of the fifth sub-plane of the Cosmic Physical Plane, for the Fifth Ray forms the substance of the entire mental plane.

It manifests in three ways as:

1. Abstract Mind or the Higher Mind;

2. Concrete or the Lower Mind, the highest aspect of the Lower Self;

3. the Son of Mind, the Soul, the point of unification showing intelligence, abstract or concrete.

Just as the personality functions as a medium for Soul expression, so the Concrete Mind acts as a channel for the inflow of higher mental energy. Called "The Door into the Mind of God," the Fifth Ray is extremely influential in Taurus because it is the agency for developing consciousness, the cosmic goal for our solar system. It is *latent* energy when awaiting usage; *dynamic,* when functioning as the agent for making thought-forms.

The First Ray of Will or Power emphasizes the will-to-illumine which in its destroying aspect brings about the death of form so that the Soul may be free to move forward on the Path of Evolution. Its drive urges man to mount to greater heights of spiritual understanding stressing the power to illumine Divine Purpose which will be implemented by the working out of the Plan. At the moment the human mind is too limited to understand the nature of Cosmic Purpose. But like electricity, whose nature is still to be defined and fully explored its manifestation can be recognized and studied with greater understanding by certain of its indications appearing in the unfolding pattern of the Plan.

THE PLANETS

Venus. Goddess of Love and Beauty, she is the exoteric ruler of Taurus and is the sole carrier-agent of the Fifth Ray. Her influence is always tinged with mental quality. Here in the sign of the Bull she is concerned with the development of the personality in its early stages of growth, when its baser instincts are stimulated toward gratification of the senses. When satiety is reached in this area, the next search is directed toward the "aesthetic" and this, too, becomes only a stepping stone to a still unsatisfied longing. The search is finally turned inward to a still higher level seeking fulfillment; this new direction marks an approach to the Soul and the beginning of contact with it.

Venus is associated with sex and in the Wisdom Teaching comment makes it clear that when the expression of sex on the physical plane is restrained it is considered to be "right," but when prostituted or perverted it is "wrong." The union of male and female on the physical level is symbolic of the higher relationship of the marriage of Spirit and Matter, itself a basic expression of the Law of Attraction.

Vulcan. God of the Hammer and Forge, Vulcan is both the esoteric and hierarchical ruler of Taurus. He continually strikes with the power of the First Ray, beating "base metal" into a more refined state to be used for spiritual purposes. His unrelenting force symbolizes the persistency needed to clear the way for Soul experience in the world of form. This legendary blacksmith performs his duty on the higher planes in order that the Soul can make progress on its own line of evolution as it gains the needed experience of knowing God manifested on a lower level of existence.

Self-Actualization and Self-Realization

The task of Self-Actualization and Self-Realization is a particularly hard one for the Taurean because it involves so many limitations that need to be overcome. Form life, intelligent activity and intense struggle summarize his problem. He must dissipate glamour and illusion before he can reach the domain of the Higher Self; however, once having reached it he can escape future deception of Truth.

Although he will go through periods of discouragement when he feels he is not achieving his goal, his depression can be overridden if he will only remember that the weaknesses of his senses lie within himself and it is his own *receiving apparatus* that is the trouble maker. This condition can be overcome if he will realize that his potentials are waiting to be developed and will be of benefit if he will only nurture them.

• • •

In relation to the physical body Taurus rules the neck and throat. The unattractive characteristic bull-neck of its subjects is often an asset, for it gives strong vocal chords to singers and power of speech to orators.

Like Mother Earth, the Taurean has stability because his roots go deep into the soil. His humor also keeps close to the ground. His love of family, friends and home is strong evidence of the Venus touch, as is his love of the beautiful. The underdeveloped type shows possessiveness and a clinging to the material things of life. Like the Bull, he has sturdy strength and a temper kept hidden until his back is pushed against the wall. When angered, he charges with unsuspected ferocity, "energy run wild in the interest of the personality."

Tenacity, endurance and stubbornness reflect qualities of the Will and, like all forces, have both a positive and a negative aspect. The hammer of Vulcan in action brings forth perseverance, persistence and power, all denoting the mark of the First Ray. In witnessing the expression of the Will, it is very necessary to recognize the *motivation* coloring the frame of reference. Take stubbornness, for example: Little Billy, a small "monster", will use his bull-headedness with intolerable selfishness, stepping on anything in the way of what he wants. However, this trait is highly praised when displayed by the mature man striving unselfishly to serve the common good.

It is obvious that exaggerated self-interest and self-esteem block the vision that leads to wisdom. If the aspiration is spasmodic it traps the intelligence and hinders knowledge from developing in a practical way the Taurean disciple needs to maintain a steady approach in order to progress on the narrow "razor-edged path" of spiritual unfoldment. Help can be reached to overcome his weaknesses if he will constantly affirm that *his is a Soul, a Son of God, who is a Son of Mind.* He can transmute undesirable traits into constructive ones if he will use the *Vulcan force* to destroy old habits and "fashion" new ones to support what he is essentially, the Transpersonal Self.

Two Taurean keywords telescope the journey of evolution:

The personality asserts: *Let struggle be undismayed.*

The Soul sounds its note: *I see, and when the eye is opened, all is illumined.*

The illumination that arrives after hard struggle is attributed to the influence of Vulcan substituting for the Sun, Logos, the Giver of Light.

Will, basic to activity in Taurus, should be the pure joyful will which needs to be expressed in service to others—the will-to-good transformed into goodwill. The nature of Will is admitted to be a mystery and more and more today psychiatrists are probing to understand it. Roberto Assagioli, in his book, *The Act of Will,* offers many ideas on the subject and describes the will in one aspect as being:

> ...a small but distinct voice sometimes making itself heard, urging us to a specific course of action, a prompting which is different from that of our ordinary motives and impulses. We feel that it comes from the central core of our being. Or else an inner illumination makes us aware of the *reality* of the will, with overwhelming conviction that asserts itself irresistably.
>
> The discovery of the will in oneself, and even more the realization that the self (Soul) and will are intimately connected, may come as a real revelation which can change, often radically, a man's self-awareness and his whole attitude towards himself, other people, or the world. He perceives that he is a 'living subject' endowed with the power to choose, to relate, to bring about changes in his own personality, in others, in circumstances. This enhanced awareness, this 'awakening' and vision of new unlimited potentialities for inner expression and outer action, gives a

new feeling of confidence, security and joy—a sense of 'wholeness'...

The most effective and satisfying role of the will is not as a source of *direct power* or force, but as that function which, being at our command, can stimulate, regulate and direct all other functions and forces of our being so that they may lead us to our predetermined goal...

The function of the will is similar to that performed by the helmsman of a ship. He knows what the ship's course should be, and keeps her steady on it, despite the drift caused by the wind and current. But the power he needs to turn the wheel is altogether different from that required to propel the ship through the water, whether it be generated by engines, the pressure of the winds on the sail, or the effort of a rower...

Let us realize thoroughly the full meaning and immense value of the discovery of the will...in whatever way it happens, either spontaneously or through conscious action, in a crisis or in the quiet of inner recollection, it constitutes a most important decisive event in our lives.*

● ● ●

To reiterate, "form life, intelligent activity and intense struggle" summarize the Taurean problem which demands a recognition of the reality lying behind the deceptive facade of events which are met in daily livingness. This can be achieved when the light of the Transpersonal Self illumines the vision; then the man can stand tall and look far.

Persons born under the sign of the Bull often lack an indication of the Second Ray of Love—Wisdom in their make-up and this may be explained by the fact that there is too much focussing on the little self and its desires.

Analysis shows that a person can be intelligent but not wise, aspirational but at the same time stubborn, so much so that his aspiration does not carry him very far in development with any rapidity for his tendency is to rush forward in "spurts." Steadiness for him is hard to acquire; it is also difficult to practically apply the knowledge he has gained, for often he will let it remain merely a

*The Act of Will, p. 7, 9, 10, 47.

mental acquisition. He will realize the "existence of duality," but instead of the realization making him struggle all the harder for unity, it acts as a depressant and creates a static condition.

The man who aspires to move forward on the path of spiritual unfoldment must, under this sign, grasp the spiritual side of Venus, appreciate the value of love, and, at the same time, renounce the destructive side of Vulcan and focus on its power to develop what he truly is—The Self. This demands clear seeing, *joyful willingness* and death of personality desires in toto.

GEMINI, THE TWINS
May 21 - June 21

Gemini, the third sign in the zodiac, is one of the most important of the twelve, for its influence lies behind every one of them.

Its function is to deal with all the pairs of opposites keeping the relationships fluid so that eventually there is fusion and synthesis creating a final unity. Sometimes this sign of the Twins is referred to as the *constellation of the resolution of duality into fluid synthesis.*

One of its applications is to relate the six pairs of polar opposite signs that lie 180 degrees apart on the zodiacal wheel. Governing all of them, it maintains the magnetic interplay of their energies which develops a *fusion in consciousness* that finally transmutes the twelve into six—the ultimate goal. This offers a great advantage to the advanced initiate who, with developed intuitive sensitivity, has both individual and universal consciousness which enables him to "partake of the freedom of the two."

In the long journey of experience in *form*, the activity of the Gemini man is mainly carried on unconsciously; however this condition is changed when the Soul exerts its influence on the personality and spiritual unfoldment takes place on a higher level. Two keywords give the pattern:

The personality asserts: *Let instability do its work.*

The Soul proclaims: *I recognize my other self and in the waning of that self, I grow and glow.*

Separativeness is the hallmark of the personality which exists for a very long period characterized by changeableness and vacillation; but finally these traits are modified by the activity of the Soul which effects the balancing of the opposites.

The twin stars, Castor and Pollux, represent the Gemini symbol. According to legend, these were the sons of Jupiter and Leda, Queen of Sparta. In a quarrel, Castor was killed and Pollux became so grief-stricken by the separation that Jupiter, to assuage his suffering, transformed the brothers into celestial lights and placed them in the heavens where they never again would be separated.

The life of the Father (Spirit and Will) flowing through both twins makes them one in reality, although they are two in manifestation. Their real nature as "the elder brother and the Prodigal Son" is revealed by the intuition when it takes hold of the mind and activates the will-to-relate that resolves the conflict between spirit and matter. Nevertheless, in the last analysis, it is the will-to-love which finally governs the relationship and establishes synthesis.

It is comforting and encouraging to learn that Gemini produces those changes needed for the evolution of the Christ consciousness (Soul consciousness) at any point in time and space; it is always compatible with the requirement.

Gemini is an air sign, the third in the triplicity of Libra and Aquarius. It rules the lungs, the nervous system, the oxygenation of the blood, and arms and hands.

One of its most important relationships is with the nervous system whose underlying energy structure is the *Etheric Body*, a network of myriad lines of universal energy composed of the substance *prana* which substands all bodies in all kingdoms of nature. This cosmic energy comprises the *True Form*, the skeleton foundation for the visible bodies that we recognize.

In regard to the human being, this etheric body is a subjective form, the third vehicle of the personality which the Soul brings into existence in the beginning of its experience in "Matter." *Its main function is to communicate.*

It plays several roles. One, it transmits vital pranic energy which galvanizes the outer dense body into healthful activity; it carries the health-giving prana from the Sun. Two, it relays impressions from the three bodies to each other; mental, emotional and etheric; when a certain degree of personality integration has been achieved, the Higher Self uses it to transmit its own quality via the mind to the brain.

The *etheric* system is of such great magnitude that its interlocking channels of force form lines of communication throughout the universe, even from atom to star. It links all forms of manifestation. In a human being the intersection of etheric lines of force create vortices of energy which have their counterparts in the dense physical body as the endocrine glands. And since the glands affect the blood stream and "the blood is the life," the etheric is not only connected with the consciousness aspect of man, but with the life force as well.

Due to this extraordinary pattern the disciple can begin to grasp some understanding of the mechanism of the processes which are making him be what he is.

Cosmic Rays and Planetary Rulers

THE RAYS

The Second Ray of Love-Wisdom, the all powerful basic ray of our solar system, passes through Gemini and emphasizes the omnipresence of the Love of God.

> God is that Whose Center is everywhere
> And Whose Periphery is nowhere.
> —Plato

Ray Two along with Ray One and Ray Three form the three major influences, and Love-Wisdom manifests the cosmic principle of love through fusion, attraction and cohesion. It shows the relation of Love and Will as it expresses an indefinable power that passes between Spirit and Matter and draws them together into a blended whole indicating the activity of *Will functioning through Love.*

Besides the Second, three other Rays are influential in this sign of the Twins—the Fourth exoterically, the Fifth esoterically and the Third hierarchically.

The Fourth Ray of Harmony through Conflict, having acted as an esoteric influence in Aries, now in Gemini exhibits its power exoterically by creating conflict and struggle for the personality, which will challenge man's potentials as it furnishes experiences necessary for the transmutation and transformation of the lower self. Under the continual drive of this ray personality desires become weaker, and with their appeal lessened, the way for the Soul to take control is gradually opened.

The Fifth Ray of Concrete Knowledge or Science is pre-eminently the substance of the entire mental plane. Its nature is gaseous therefore its quality is volatile. It is easily dispersed and is the receptive agent for illumination. In the preceding sign of Taurus its influence was on the exoteric life, but in Gemini, oriented Soul-ward, it is on the esoteric. It is considered to be the most potent energy due to the fact that its power was matured in the first solar system where it became the key to Universal Mind. Now, when fused with Love, it emerges as Love-Wisdom illustrating the interpretation that "wisdom is knowledge gained by experience and implemented by love." This Fifth Ray is exceedingly responsive to impulses of various kinds and in reacting to them creates thought-forms. Its activity transforms divine ideas into human ideals and it is seen working through science, philosophy and psychology. Its expression is often distorted, but it works steadily toward illumination and its effect down the ages is shown in civilizations and cultures.

The Third Ray of Active Intelligence in Gemini implements the work of the Second Ray so that love may be applied intelligently. This Ray will be discussed in detail in a later section.

THE PLANETS

Mercury. Its job in Gemini, as the exoteric ruler, differs from the one it has in Aries where it casts its influence esoterically. Here in the sign of the Twins it focusses the strength of the Fourth Ray on the personality, constantly providing those challenges which will make it a more acceptable instrument for Soul use. Mercury is the Mediator, and in relating soul to personality it functions as the illuminating mind.

Venus in the preceding sign of Taurus acts as the exoteric ruler striving to develop the personality, but in Gemini her endeavor is reversed. Her energy is focussed on the Higher Self bringing in the forces of spiritual will. It is through her activity that the more evolved man begins to understand and express the higher faculties of his nature. It is in Gemini that he first begins to have some embryonic understanding of causes and effects of the Plan, and when he becomes an enlightened disciple of an advanced stage, he receives understanding that emanates from the plane of Love-Wisdom, revealing how the Fifth and Second Ray are closely related.

Venus and our planet Earth are also closely related, for in time immemorial when Great Beings arrived on our globe and sparked the minds of animal men,* the planet Venus also received great stimulus and is often spoken of as the earth's alter ego. These two planets are mutually influential but Venus, being further along in systemic development, has the rank of a "sacred" planet while the Earth, at a lower level on the cosmic ladder, is classified as a "non-sacred" one.

It has been prophesized that in the future, during the Aquarian Age, Venus will play a very important role in stimulating group consciousness. Individual consciousness, formerly the focus for growth, will be over shadowed by emphasis on a form of group individualism affecting all mankind.

The Earth, as the hierarchical ruler, along with the Third Ray will be discussed in the analysis of Sagittarius, the polar opposite of Gemini.

Self-Actualization and Self-Realization

The foremost problem confronting the Gemini individual seeking identification with the Higher, Transpersonal Self lies in the control of mind over emotions and the physical body. This must be achieved in order to develop an integrated personality (Actualization) and the final synthesis of Body and Soul (Self-Realization).

What we know about life and what we feel about it do not dwell in regular separate compartments. The wall

*These Great Beings, called the Lords of the Flame, came from an area related to Venus. Details for the cosmological background can be found in *A Treatise on Cosmic Fire* by Alice A. Bailey.

between them is porous. They flow into each other, so that new knowledge tends to induce some new response; and conversely, a "change of heart" often prompts a search for new knowledge.*

The needed mental control can be developed through the influence of Mercury which in activating the mind to dispel glamour and illusion, permits the personality to be free from these chains and ready to acquiesce to Soul impression. It is through the willingness of the personality that sublimation can take place and create "the new man in Christ".

Sensitivity and quick reaction are marked Gemini characteristics which are in parallel with restlessness and indecision. Astrologer Ellen McCaffrey acknowledges the need here for perseverance that will furnish the means to overcome this restlessness so often exhibiting a lack of a centralized life purpose that results in following too many paths to too many goals.

Florence Jensen, writing in *Horoscope* Magazine points out that "Gemini is always facile, adapts easily to quickly changing circumstances and can side-step issues on the spur of the moment...because its mental quality is lacking in warmth, it tends to outwit others in quite a calculating way..."**

Those born under the Sign of the Twins can speak well and write well and because of the dual nature of Gemini, flexibility and dexterity are among its assets.

Adaptability, mutability, pervasiveness, rapidity, intelligence and intuition are all listed as characteristics, but there is ever the need for the intuition to over-ride the mercurial qualities of the Gemini nature.

Those who are born under this sign are said to be affectionate, but sometimes hide their feelings under a misunderstood attitude of shyness. Their need is both physical and psychical and a helpful means to acquire the "psychic" condition is described by the Overstreets as the creation of "psychic" space—this is an area which makes room for thoughts and feelings, something that we must make first for ourselves before we can make it for others. This is the power to treat life as "roomy" rather than cramped, and

*The Mind Goes Forth, page 80.
**Horoscope magazine, June 1973, page 100.

will show in our attitude. It reveals, in short, something quite basic about ourselves.

"People need to recognize and acknowledge their praise-worthy thoughts and emotions so that they can manage them while they are still manageable...People need to turn around when they find themselves going in the wrong direction, they need psychic space in which to correct errors—and move beyond them."*

For the undeveloped man, gaining mental control sometimes evokes violent outbursts of emotions but this is one of the necessary experiences which have to be overcome in order to conquer the vacillating quality of the Gemini type. It is admitted that pain and struggle accompany growth and at the time of occurence are often resented. However, when recognized later in its true light, the experience is appreciated as a means of release for awareness on a level higher than the place of occurrence.

In the Gemini pattern of conflict between the pairs of opposites, the interplay of energies between Body and Soul reaches the final goal of fusion which irradiates light that is recognized by other Souls. Teilhard de Chardin writes meaning-fully of this when he says:

> Human beings are drawn together not merely under the pressure of external forces, or merely by the performance of material acts, but directly, centre to centre, through internal attraction.**

According to one psychological interpretation, the interplay of the energies of the opposites creates an intermediate state known as *ambivalance*, which is a seemingly contradictory situation when we are simultaneously attracted and repulsed by the same person or object. However, this reaction occurs at several levels of our nature and obviously must be adjusted before *fusion* can take place. But this is only one requisite for integration. Other demands include *stabilizing* the Gemini changeableness and vacillation, *establishing* a sense of proportion in relation to right values, *slowing* mercurial quickness, *subduing* nervous

*The Mind Goes Forth, pp. 54, 56.
**The Future of Man, p. 227.

tension through a control of understanding, and *cultivating* discretion on many levels of consciousness.

Eloquence of speech and of writing comes easily to the Gemini person for he has a keen capacity for intellectual expression; his inborn sensitivity makes identification with his true inner Self express a liberal attitude and reflect the Transpersonal Self. True worth is recognized when the disciple has gone through many life experiences and knows the significance of consciousness. His insight arrives with his intuitive perception and a realization of the essential one-ness underlying the illusion of the twin brothers seen as a duality, but which in reality are a unity which has been brought into existence by the will-to-love—that which creates the final synthesis.

"Fluidity, recognition of duality, soul control...are the keynotes...of your life for whether you are in this sign (Gemini) in this life, it has at some time and many times conditioned your experience, and the results are marked in the life of the advanced disciple."*

*Esoteric Astrology, p. 370.

CANCER, THE CRAB
June 21 - July 21

"I build a lighted house and therein dwell."*

    Cancer is said to be one of the most difficult signs of the zodiac to understand since its basic theme is *Form* and for aeons Form controls and hides the Soul.

    The sign of the Crab is "one of the signs of synthesis and of relative fusion, but it is a fusion on the lower level of the spiral and connotes the fusion of the physical body and the soul but only in the embryonic stage and with the psychic stage still unindividualised...

    "Soul light affects the form as evolution proceeds and produces sequentially the revelation of that form. It is said that the whole story of Astrology revolves around the story of form, for it is the building of forms and their use by the Soul, which makes possible its spiritual growth on levels lower than its own; and by so doing it gains experience through matter thus fulfilling an essential part of the divine plan; for it is explained that without the need to respond sensitively to the conditions and circumstances (that matter presents) the Soul would never awaken to the knowledge in the three worlds and therefore never know God in manifestation...it is the irradiation of matter and growth of the

Esoteric Astrology, p. 343.

light body within the macrocosm or microcosm that finally makes clear the purpose of the Logos..."*

As the personality grows it sounds its note through these keywords:

Let isolation rule and yet the crowd exists. The word "crowd" gives the clue to the type of early Cancerian consciousness of embryonic instinctual awareness, conditioned by mass conscious-ness which rules it and sways its judgement. For many incarnations a man is not a personality but only a member of the mass.

Cancer symbolizes the will of the masses which, viewed psychologically, is seen as a coherent unit emerging as public opinion. It is not often that the herd instinct is thought of in the light of synthesis. In this section of the zodiac it is demonstrated on a low level where the thinking of the crowd, unified into a whole, creates a singularly powerful force causing any individual expression to be only a reflection of it.

Conscious identification of the Soul with its personality during this stage is practically non-existent. The aspect of the Soul which is concealed within the sheaths of form is, for a long, long period, dominated by the life of those sheaths, making its presence felt only through "the voice of conscience". But as time goes on it works slowly from its own plane and eventually brings about the integration of these lower bodies into a functioning whole—the personality.

The most powerful of all influences that dominate at this time are the astral and they remain in control for a very long period. Cancer is a water sign (with Scorpio and Pisces) and reflects the emotional quality that water symbolizes. When "feelings and desires" clash with the physical forces, conflict gives rise to glamour, a condition so difficult to dissipate when clear vision of truth is needed. Eventually immersion in herd consciousness gradually disappears for the Soul produces "the growth of light in Light" that opens up new fields of awareness, and the "I" consciousness of the personality faintly asserts itself and stands apart from the mass to nourish its individuation.

Resistance to the organized mass can be affected only by the man who is as well organized in his individuality as the mass itself.*

*Esoteric Astrology, p. 329-330.

** Carl Jung, The Undiscovered Self, p. 60.

The personality life of the co-ordinated individual for a large number of lives falls into three phases where the man is:

a. dominant, aggressive, selfish and very individualistic;

b. in a transitional stage where conflict rages between the personality and the Soul seeking liberation from the personality;

c. controlled by the Soul leading to the final death and destruction of the personality when the light of the Soul obliterates the light of matter (complete infusion) and the personality is completely identified with the Soul. This is a renewal of the phase of previous identification of Soul with the personality—for now the two have become "one."*

Cancer is said to be concerned primarily with the world of causes, and it is the inner meanings and subtleties that escape recognition which are hard to understand.

"In Cancer, God breathed into man's nostrils the breath of life and man became a living soul. In these words you have established the relation which exists in the mind of God between spirit (the breath of life), the soul (consciousness) and man (the form)...

...In *Aries*, the essential substance of manifestation awoke to renewed activity under the impact of divine desire, impelled by the divine Breath, by divine Life or Spirit. In *Cancer*, this living substance assumed a triple differentiated relationship known as Life (Aries), Consciousness (Taurus) and manifested Duality (Gemini)...These three blended together came into outer expression in this fourth sign of the zodiac, Cancer, thus completing an esoteric quaternary of great importance."**

Cosmic Rays and Planetary Rulers

THE RAYS

Sensitivity, so dominant a characteristic in the nature of the Cancerian, is nourished by two rays, the Fourth and the Sixth. Care must be taken to prevent becoming over-sensitive.

* *Esoteric Healing*, p. 505-507.
** *Esoteric Astrology*, p. 313-14.

The *Fourth Ray of Harmony through Conflict*, creating situations that present struggle, has a different mission here than it has in Aries. There it was oriented toward aiding the Soul esoterically; here it goads the personality into more acute reactions, a constant challenge to its being controlled by mass consciousness in which it is imbedded. In Cancer it works toward eventually releasing the man from the bonds of form in which the mass mind holds him. Over and over again the engendered conflict moves toward an increasing harmony which will make this possible.

Meanwhile the Soul, during inordinate time, keeps throwing its light into its personality vehicle and proclaims the keywords: *I build a lighted house and therein dwell.*

The *Sixth Ray of Devotion or Idealism*, also in contrast to its activity in Aries where it motivates exoterically, now heightens spiritual unfoldment, nourishing Soul progress by increasing high aspiration (devotion to an idea or ideal), widening the man's vision and opening up the way for the intuition to descend from its lofty environment, carrying touches of the higher perception of Love-Wisdom.

THE PLANETS

The Moon. As the exoteric ruler, the Moon plays an unusual role in this sign of the Crab for, besides presenting challenges for growth by carrying Fourth Ray impulsing, it works toward integrating the personality, helping to protect it from an overwhelming bombardment of impacts. It does this by failing to register or step down many of the impacts to which the true man is sensitive. Average humanity is not fully equipped to bear the full range of these contacts, to handle them constructively or to transmute them and interpret them accurately.

The Moon veils the planet Neptune for the mass mind but this does not apply to the disciple working toward spiritual unfoldment. One of his great difficulties and major problems is "extra sensitivity" to impressions and the rapidity with which he responds to them as they come from "all points of the compass."

The material of which the earth is composed is of a thick, coarse quality, heavy and dull; the objective of the Moon influencing "form" is to refine it. This it does over a long period of transition with struggle and conflict arising to give challenges for growth; the refinement is finally accomplished and the material made effective for Soul use.

Neptune, God of the Sea, Poseidon, rules Cancer esoterically. His power is felt only after the disciple has made some headway in spiritual being and is not blinded by the glamour* and illusion** which this planet creates for those who are unable to recognize deceit. But for the spiritually advanced, this ruler enlarges vision, leading aspiration to the high level of the Buddhic plane where intuitive perception brings true insight.

Self-Actualization and Self-Realization

In this sign of the Crab the particular need is to lift the consciousness from the astral to the mental plane, where the mind can dominate the emotional habits long and deeply ingrained, as well as any other super-sensitive reactions that hinder spiritual progress. When inner pressures begin to plague they must be faced squarely, and when the man is confronted by a problem he must stand steady and look to the Higher Self for that guidance which will help him find the solution for his dilemma. The individual must develop those responses which will automatically lift him out of any mass mind influence; he has to stand alone and recognize his self-hood, a stage of development to be carried forward in the following sign of Leo.

The Cancerian needs to see himself in many relationships including his relation to his family, to friends, and groups of all kinds. When his vision has been extended he will be able to gain perspective on himself and particularly appreciate that he is a part of a greater Whole. His job is to affect a synthesis of his physical, emotional and mental bodies, realizing that there must be some changes made and which of his negative traits must be transmuted into more desirable characteristics. Goethe once said that harmony of life comes not to him who attains his goals, but to him who ceaselessly striving, bestirs himself.

Cancer rules the breast, stomach, the region of the abdomen, the intestines and diaphragm, the area of the solar plexus which in

Veiled truth on the astral plane.
*Veiled truth on the mental plane.

the undeveloped man is the center of his lower desires. Like the Crab, the Cancerian is very tenacious and this is revealed on many levels. It is very hard for him to pry loose from his desires, but once they have been transformed into an expression of some higher value they become a treasured asset.

Gordon Allport sees *Desire* in a broad frame of reference, not within the usual limitations of baser aspects of the emotions, and his comments cast fresh enlightenment in this area: "Faith," he says, "is basically man's belief in the validity and attainability of some goal (value). The goal is not set by desires. Desires, however, are not merely pushes from behind (drive-ridden). They include such complex, future-oriented states as longing for a better world, for one's perfection, for a completely satisfying relation to the universe. So important is this forward thrust in all desires emanating from mature sentiments that I propose the term 'intention' to depict the dynamic operation we are endeavoring to describe. Better than 'desire' the term designates the presence of the rational and ideational component in all productive striving. Some sort of idea of the end is always bound into the act itself. It is this inseparability of the idea of the end from the course of the striving that we call faith."*

The Cancer man or woman can be very moody and when conditions do not suit them they seek solitude; keen sensitivity makes them easily hurt as well as easily responsive to psychism, high or low depending on their points of evolution. Lower psychism pulls down glamour and when the thinking is that of the crowd they take its opinion as their own and revert to the prejudice of the masses.

However, this sensitivity is the very factor that provides them with fertile imaginations and the world of fantasy they evoke when they are blinded by the unreality that the astral visions create with strong appeal. Sometimes this produces an emphasis which gives them a sense of false importance and they evaluate their psychic sense as that which makes them mediums for the expression of ideas from the Higher Worlds.

To balance their liabilities, Cancerians are endowed with affectionate natures, desirable, retentive memories (the tenacity of the Crab) whose camera-like qualities quickly absorb and then

*The Individual and His Religion, p. 130-131.

reflect. There is a strong maternal instinct in their natures, and shyness is often misinterpreted as haughtiness. Cancerians will fight for their ideals.

When they have overcome fear of knowing their weaknesses, they have, relatively speaking, taken a "giant step" toward the goal of Self-Realization.

Abraham Maslow throws much light on the value of self-knowledge in his book, *Towards a Psychology of Being,* where he analyzes "The Need to Know and the Fear of Knowing":

> From our point of view, Freud's greatest discovery is that *the* great cause of much psychological illness is the fear of knowledge of oneself—of one's emotions, impulses, memories, capacities, potentialities, one's destiny...

> In general this kind of fear is defensive, in the sense that it is a protection of our self-esteem, of our love and respect for ourselves. We tend to be afraid of any knowledge that could cause us to despise ourselves or to make us feel inferior, weak, worthless, evil, shameful. We protect ourselves and our ideal image of ourselves by repression and similar defenses, which are essentially techniques by which we avoid becoming conscious of unpleasant or dangerous truths... ("To be completely honest with oneself is the very best effort a human being can make." S. Freud.)

> But there is another kind of truth we tend to evade... a denying of our best side, of our talents, of our finest impulses, of our highest potentialities, of our creativeness. In brief this is the struggle against our own greatness, the fear of *hubris*...

> ...to discover in oneself a great talent can certainly bring exhilaration but it also brings a fear of the dangers and responsibilities and duties of being a leader and of being all alone. Responsibility can be seen as a heavy burden and evaded as long as possible...

> The adult human being is... subtle and concealed about his anxieties and fears. If they do not overwhelm him

altogether, he is very apt to repress them, to deny even to himself that they exist. Frequently, he does not "know" that he is afraid.

...One way of rendering them familiar, predictable, manageable, controllable, i.e., unfrightening, and harmless, is to know them and to understand them. And so knowledge may have not only a growing-forward function, but also an anxiety-reducing function, a protective homeostatic function...

The anxiety-free person can be more bold and more courageous and can explore and theorize for the sake of knowledge itself. It is certainly reasonable to assume that the latter is more likely to approach the truth, the real nature of things...*

It is in the constant be-stirring of himself that the Cancerian reaches the heights of spiritual unfoldment. And when on the Path of Discipleship he seeks to aid his fellowmen and reincarnates under the sign of the Crab, he becomes a valuable server of humanity for he then serves the masses in a consciousness of love.

*Towards a Psychology of Being, Second Edition, 1968, p. 60, 61, 64, 65.

LEO, THE LION
July 24 - August 23

There is no need to run outside
For better seeing.
Nor to peer from a window. Rather abide
At the center of your being;
For the more you leave it, the less you learn.
Search your heart and see
If he is wise who takes each turn;
The way to do is the way to be.*

—Lao Tzu

Leo is of primary importance in the development of consciousness, for here with the Lion of Self-Assertion emerges the first appearance of individuality. It is in this fifth sign of the zodiac that the awkening of self-consciousness begins; the moving-out from the instinctual collective consciousness of the herd, which is characteristic of Cancer, into a recognition of a personal Self.

As a "first step on a journey of a thousand miles," it leads to that growth of the personality which slowly expresses the self-actualizing process where the blending of the thinking, feeling and vital parts of a man's constitution produces the synthesis of

*The Way of Life, from a translation by Witter Bynner.

the lower self into an integrated whole. As Carl Jung points out, "the development of the personality is synonymous with an increase of awareness."*

It is said that in Leo there is that power to go forth and touch that which is desired, and this is the basis of all sense of awareness or that responsiveness which characterizes the underlying sense of progress—the evolutionary movement forward. Here lies the keynote of achieving the true self-centered attitude that makes a man an individual.

> Personality is less a finished product than a transitive process. While it has some stable features, it is at the same time continually undergoing a course of change—that of becoming individuation.**

According to the Ageless Wisdom, self-identity, a hallmark of the young Leo, is the accumulation of special crises brought about by the will-to-be and the will-to-manifest as they increase self-consciousness. The pattern of unfoldment reveals first the stage of inchoate, diffused power and then personality integration. Meanwhile, the will-to-illumine increases the drive toward self-knowledge, the will-to-rule-and-dominate evokes the attitude of the personality which proclaims its keyword: *I rule because I am.*

The young Leo is not interested in any higher consciousness and therefore is not aware of the Soul. But when changes have altered this self-centered perspective and some measure of spirituality is awakened, the man becomes aware of his motivating impulses and begins to redirect his endeavors toward unselfish objectives. This is accomplished by self-imposed discipline and denial which engender conflict with the little self and finally results in the personality becoming subservient to the Soul. This new reorientation brings a release from the idea of being an isolated individual. With this realization the aspirant recognizes that there are needs to be filled other than his own and he happily goes forth to serve some group or groups.

This "Lion" is considered the most material of all the signs for its selfish objectives present the "battleground of the Forces of Materialism and the Forces of Light." There is the period when his

*The Integration of the Personality, p. 302.
**Becoming, p. 19.

intense possessiveness sweeps everything aside with violent control. This occurs before the power of the higher forces can dominate and free him from his insatiable desires and lead him to humanitarian service.

• • •

Leo is the second in the triplicity of the fire signs with Aries and Sagittarius.

Fire is a cleansing agent and can purify the personality vehicles. A symbolic illustration of this is found in the book of Daniel (3; 25) where Shadrach, Mesach and Abednego are in the fiery furnace. These represent the mental, emotional and physical bodies under a test which, along with the soul, are described in the Bible as:

> Lo, I see four men loose, walking in the midst of fire and they have no hurt; and the form of the fourth is like the Son of God.

Alice A. Bailey picks up the thread of the story in her book, *From Intellect to Intuition,* where she significantly points out that there is no escaping from the fiery furnace of purification but the reward is commensurate with the trial. "We start", she says, "with an emotional realization of our goal and from then, pass on through the fire of discipline to the heights of intellectual certainty..."*

The old aphorism, *ignis santa,* applies, and the personality must endure the test of the "burning ground," that character-building may be an ongoing process.

Folk tales often carry a subtle meaning and the old nursery rhyme of the Lion and the Unicorn *going up to town* is an instance where surface meaning hides a symbolic significance. The Lion (Leo) and the Unicorn (Capricorn)—the legendary beast of purity and the highest symbol of Capricorn—travel together toward the town (the fifth kingdom of Souls). Personality and Soul in the "going-up" approach the door of admittance to the Spiritual Hierarchy of the planet. In the myth the Personality is conquered when the heart of the Lion is pierced by the single horn of the Unicorn; the Higher self controls the lower and the first major

*p. 94.

initiation is taken with entrance into the "Heart of God"—the Hierarchy.

Sensitivity is the key to the Leo activity and like the Sun standing in the center of his system, so man stands in his own center, small as his little universe may appear. As a self-conscious unit he responds to various impacts which include first his underdeveloped personality, later his integrated one. Still later, the Soul acts as a conditioning factor and finally the man responds as a "God-Man," the fused personality and Soul.

Cosmic Rays and Planetary Rulers

THE RAYS

Three rays dominate in this sign: The Second Ray of Love-Wisdom, The Sixth Ray of Devotion or Idealism and the Seventh Ray of Ceremonial Order or Magic. All pass through the Sun before reaching the earth. The Sun's own ray is the Second, the Sixth is channeled by Neptune which is veiled by the Sun, and Uranus transmits the Seventh, also veiled by the Sun. In its triple activity the Sun is a three-in-one ruler, exoteric, esoteric and hierarchical.

It is postulated that the purpose of this solar system is the unfoldment of consciousness, hence the concentrated influence of the Sun where human consciousness is concerned.

The stimulation of consciousness is, we are told, the objective of all astrological signs, and it follows that Leo highlights this central theme with self-consciousness being developed as a result of sensitive response to environmental impacts.

The Second Ray. The Dual aspect of this ray may be clarified by examining the meaning of love and wisdom.

Love is the great cohesive force that develops all the divine attributes of the Kingdom of God during evolution; it builds the structure for the expression of spirit. It has the power to attract and magnetize, and in so doing evokes both a negative and positive aspect where the destructive aspect expresses separativeness and a hindrance to spiritual growth. On its positive side, it opens the way to the higher evolution. It illustrates the Law of Attraction.

Wisdom, defined in special esoteric context, is the *understanding achieved through the intuition,* where intuition indicates higher knowledge over and above the reasoning mind. It displays inclusiveness and identification in the human being.

Maurice Maeterlinck makes a meaningful distinction between the two:

> This thing is reasonable and this thing is wisdom... reason and love contrast violently at first within the Soul that elevated itself, but wisdom is born of the final reconcilation of love and reason...The more reason yields its prerogatives to love, the more perfect is this peace. The deeper the love becomes, the wiser it gets, the more wisdom elevates, the closer it approaches love. Love and you will become wiser, become wiser, and you will out of necessity grow into love. One only loves truly by becoming better, and to become better is to become more wise.*

The Sixth Ray of Devotion or Idealism with its characteristic energy, is met first in Aries and later in Cancer. It is a subsidiary of the Third Ray of Active Intelligence and expresses devotion to some objective high or low. For the conservative or one who clings to the conventional, it becomes the line of least resistance, but it should not be denigrated for it serves a valuable purpose as a steadying influence to restrain overenthusiasm and hasty judgment.

In Leo it accentuates self-centeredness. On the lower level, in relation to the love expressed by the Second Ray, it stimulates desire of a base quality, animal passion, which in a later development becomes transmuted into the higher expression of love for family, friends, country, or even universal love.

The Seventh Ray of Ceremonial Order and Ritual is a subsidiary of the Third Ray. It is also the lowest expression of the First Ray of Will or Power. Its primary function is to relate Spirit and Matter.

In the Leo environment the Seventh Ray stimulates interest in ritual and the occult; and promotes orderliness and practicality. It brings into expression whatever vision may have been gained by the Sixth Ray and works toward fusion and synthesis.

After the aspirant has developed some spiritual unfoldment, his mind is then opened to recognition of "group" importance,

*Wisdom and Destiny, p. 668-9.

and so his aspiration is impulsed. The Seventh Ray encourages mental freedom, loving understanding and heightens the consciousness. Its main area of operation is on the physical plane where it affects changes in all forms.

THE PLANETS

The Sun. Solar energy affects the physical body by bringing vital energy to the heart; it influences the personality on the astral level conducting the force of Neptune; it stimulates the mind while veiling Uranus and emphasizes the duality of the higher and lower mind as it nurtures their fusion toward at-one-ment.

Neptune. This God of the Sea impulses the growth of mystical consciousness leading to higher vision. In man's early stages of growth, Neptune exerts a negative influence. But, after emotion-desire is transformed into love-aspiration, the baser emotions are sublimated for the Higher Self when its acute sensitive nature has become responsive to the energies coming from the "Heart of the Sun." The result is obviously positive.

Uranus. God of the Ether, the planet of occultism, reveals underlying causes which produce the outer effects; it destroys old forms to make way for incoming new paterns. Uranus is characterized by the scientific mind and spiritual consciousness in contrast to human consciousness; it provides the "burning ground experience," always working to better conditions for the exoteric life as it creates a blending of the outer and inner man.

When this planet is in control, the Leo subject is the true observer and, though detached from materialism, he uses "form" to fit his endeavors. As both an electric, dynamic leader and pioneer, he is conscious of his own identity which conditions self-awareness with abstract power. This gives him a spiritual consciousness capable of great expression. The Uranian influence makes possible *control of the mind by the Soul* and in so doing frees the man from environmental influences, thus giving him a power to be used for higher purposes.* In relation to the physical body, Leo rules the heart from which flows the life-giving quality.

*Esoteric Astrology.

Self-Actualization and Self-Realization

According to an esoteric point of view, Leo is a sign where instinctual self-consciousness is replaced by a sense of individual responsibility. Carl Jung, writing on the integration of the personality, gives a vivid description of what happens when individualization takes place:

> ...the birth of a personality has a restoring effect upon the individual. It is as if a stream that was losing itself in marshy tributaries suddenly discovered its proper bed or as if some stone that lay upon a germinating seed were suddenly lifted away so that the sprout could begin its natural growth.*

To achieve Self-Actualization and the subsequent Self-Realization, the Leo type must become more aware of not only to what degree his consciousness is centered in the "I" of the lower synthesis, but also to what degree it is *integrated*. The primary task for him is discipline, self-imposed. The key to spiritual unfoldment lies in his ability to develop this through mental control which throws into relief the motivation for his actions. All of this is a steady pursuit to increase his sensitivity.

Rollo May also heightens the meaning of self-awareness:

> ...to undertake this "venture of becoming aware of ourselves' and to discover the sources of inner strength and security which are the rewards of such a venture, let us start at the beginning by asking, What is this person, this sense of selfhood we seek?
>
> To be...means to pierce the imagination beyond what one knows at the moment...man in fulfilling himself goes through a process of "transcending himself"...this is simply one side of the basic characteristics of the growing, healthy, human being, from the moment he is enlarging his awareness of himself and his world.**

---

*The Integration of the Personality, p. 302.
**Man's Search For Himself, p. 83, 141.

The Sun rules Leo and Leo rules the heart from which the vital life-force flows. The "Lion-hearted" sustains a certain strength which manifests as magnetism. As "ruling" comes easily to him, he can become a benevolent despot or a dictator or a great humanitarian leader dedicated to serving humanity. Courage and enthusiasm accompany the warmth of his nature in which an in-born quality of leadership is a potential that can make him a future capable general.

As an extrovert he is self-assured and self-assertive, indicative of the kingly quality of his nature which the Sun intensifies and reveals both as dignity and imperiousness. Nonetheless, Leo can inspire.

With the Sun ruling the physical body, there is often displayed a liveliness and vivaciousness which at times becomes so exaggerated that it dissipates its own strength. Vanity is often revealed in Leo's make-up with arrogance along side it; he can become very obstinate and is easily deceived. His feelings are strong and his passions run high. Often he is too generous; his likes and dislikes are too pronounced; his love is easily given as he shows his desire to be loved. Too extravagant in giving affection too quickly, it is often misplaced and brings disappointment. He needs a harmonious environment and is irritated when he hasn't got it. These latter qualities all reflect the influence of the Second Ray.

Three stages are needed to unfold consciousness for "The Lion." First there is a period from the collective to the individual consciousness; second, from the "I" to the Self; third, from the individual to the group. Each period is a move forward in spiritual unfoldment. Little by little, conscious control of inner and outer crises takes place bringing recognition of the difference between his personality and the True Being, the Self.

When Self-Realization is achieved, the Soul then proclaims its keyword: *I am That and That am I.*

Each Soul has to ascertain for himself and must find out within himself, always remembering that the Kingdom of God is within, and that only those facts which are realized within the individual consciousness as truths are of any real value.

VIRGO, THE VIRGIN
August 23 - September 23

Of all the signs in the zodiac, Virgo, the sixth, is considered to have particular significance because it involves the goal of the entire evolutionary process, which is: *to shield, nurture and finally reveal the hidden spiritual reality.*

This spirituality lies in every form, but the human form is endowed in a very different way from all others and can reveal the purpose of the creative process. In Virgo, which is the gestation period, Soul Life is sensed. But, the personality hides the Christ consciousness within and in playing her dual role, the Virgin Mother not only stimulates the Soul within the form but also stimulates the informing life that lies within each atom of that form.

The process on the involutionary arc of descent into matter centers on developing the personality which, not finding fulfillment of need in the world of the senses, begins to seek inner guidance. It is at this point the Soul begins its at-one-ing process with its vehicle of expression and the mind, which is a very important factor in achieving the goal.

Depth, darkness, quiet and warmth are the background for the valley of deep experience here where secrets are unearthed and eventually brought to light. Virgo is the place for "slow, gentle yet powerful crises and periodic developments which take place in the dark and lead to the light."* Called the "womb of Time," it is where God's Plan gradually unfolds and is brought into manifestation at the appointed time, with the mind bringing the enlightenment.

Virgo, an earth sign, is the negative pole of matter to the positive pole of spirit and acts as a redemptive agent for it. This began in a previous solar system (the one preceding ours) when Matter was the dominating force whereas, in contrast, Soul or Christ Consciousness is the controlling influence at present.

In tracing the meaning of the word itself, Virgo is found to be corruption of an ancient Atlantean root name standing for the Mother principle when a Matriarchate was founded in that civilization of the past. Many legends have grown around the idea of Mother, particularly associated with Eve, Isis and Mary, whose symbolism carries these aspects:

Eve, the Mind, taking the apple of knowledge from the serpent of Matter, depicting the lure of knowledge to be emphasized in our Aryan system as experiment, experience and expression;

Isis, referring to the emotional plane, reflecting the quickening of desire which in the ancient zodiac stood for fertility, motherhood, the guardian of the child;

Mary, carrying the manifestation of creation right down to the physical plane of incarnation, where she prepares it for eventual birth.

Archives record that the Holy Spirit—the Life of the Third Aspect—played upon the Ocean of Matter (the Virgin Mary) and during aeonic time prepared that substance for use in our current system where consciousness, not the developing of substance, is the goal, with the Christ Consciousness expressing divine consciousness as the result of that relationship.**

Evolution—Creation—Growth are the three keynotes which reveal the pattern of spiritual awakening of the right relation between spirit and matter. For man there is always the freedom of choice—a freedom to make mistakes if he so wishes. The following little poem catches this idea with meaningful simplicity.

> One day, the vine,
> That climbed on God's own house

*Esoteric Astrology, p. 260.
**Esoteric Astrology, p. 253-254.

Cried, "I will not *grow.*"
And "I will *not* grow."
And "*I* will not grow."
And God leaned out His hand, and said,
"You need not." Then the vine
Fluttered its leaves and cried:
"Oh have I not permission from the Lord
And may I not begin to cease to grow?"
But the wise God had pondered on this vine;
And all the while it labored *not* to grow
It grew and grew;
And all the time God knew.

—Anonymous

Virgo is not only the period of the hidden germ of spiritual life, but it is also the period of the germ of spiritual life showing gestation in the early stages, the stage of quickened life—the stage of probationary period or *Awakening.**

Cosmic Rays and Planetary Rulers

THE RAYS

The main energies which focus on Virgo are the Fourth, the First and the Second.

The Fourth Ray of Harmony through Conflict stimulates personality growth aiming to make it a more effective vehicle for Soul expression by constantly working on the form through which the Christ Consciousness can express itself.

The First Ray of Will or Power exerts its influence here by sending forth the *will-to-be-in-form.* This is directed toward the Soul, giving it its forceful persistent stimulation which provides greater means for the awakening of the Christ Consciousness.

The Second Ray of Love-Wisdom comes to Virgo through the planet Jupiter, whose outgoing quality carries forward the quality of Love and Wisdom to the growing personality, since this planet expresses the very essence of the nature of Christ Consciousness.

*Esoteric Astrology, p. 258.

THE PLANETS

Mercury. Again this Messenger of the Gods acts as an exoteric ruler. But, in the Virgo frame of reference he emphasizes the growth of the mind that it may produce a more sensitive refined form nature. This is in sharp contrast to his activity in Gemini, where his impulsing activates the flow of energy between spirit and matter. In this situation where the form is to be developed, Mercury engenders the crises that are testing experiences, the crucibles to distill the higher qualities for the personality.

The Moon (and Vulcan). The Moon, the esoteric ruler of Virgo, veils Vulcan, who keeps hammering away with a First Ray drive and an enduring force that keeps urging the Soul to express itself in form and promote the growth of the Christ principle. Since the Moon is associated with "form," it becomes the natural choice for Vulcan's means of expression.

Jupiter, King of the gods, gives man the opportunity to "expand"—a characteristic of Jovian power. As the hierarchical ruler of Virgo, he focusses the Second Ray of Love-Wisdom on "building" so that the Love of God can manifest more easily through a finer structure.

"Will, love and harmony through conflict are the controlling forces which make man what he is and such are the governing and directing energies which use the mind (Mercury), the emotional nature, love (Jupiter) and the physical body (the Moon or esoteric will) for purposes of divine expression and manifestation....the task of Mercury in connection with humanity has gone forward most satisfactorily and has brought humanity to its present point in evolution upon the probationary path;...the energy of Vulcan is potently making its presence felt, and hence the struggle going on upon the planet between the men of will—selfish and ambitious—and the men of good-will who are desirous of the good of the whole. When the human Hierarchy is fully awakened to spiritual and not simply material possibilities, then the work of Jupiter will immediately intensify and this beneficent ruler will lead the human family into the ways of peace and progress."* The planet Jupiter will be discussed more fully in detail in the sections on Sagittarious and Aquarius.

*Esoteric Astrology, p. 263-264.

Self-Actualization and Self-Realization

Virgo sheds a great deal of light on the relationship of the actualizing process of the lower self and the awakening of the Higher Self since it nurtures both simultaneously.

Alfred Adler, in discussing human nature from a psychological point of view, points out that:

> The ability to know one's self becomes greater when one can determine the wellsprings of his activity and the dynamics of his soul. Once he has understood this, he has become a different man and can no longer escape the inevitable consequences of his knowledge...the results of experience acquire entirely new values, when the power of self-knowledge and self-criticism is still alive, and remains a living motif....
>
> The understanding of human nature seems to us indispensable to every man, and the study of its science, the most important activity of the human mind.*

Virgo is an earth sign and is part of the triad formed with Taurus and Capricorn. In relation to the physical body it rules the abdomen, the intestines and the pancreas.

When the personality is sounding its note, the call goes forth: *Let Matter reign.*

When the Soul is in control, the Word goes forth: *I am the Mother and the Child. I, God, I, Matter am.*

Perhaps the most outstanding characteristic of this sign of the Virgin in service, be it in employment, helping one's family or a friend, or, on a higher turn of the spiral, serving humanity. Where the Virgoans are not affectionate by nature and in the main prefer to serve rather than be served, they give freely of themselves, of their time and their effort. Consciousness reveals itself in their acceptance of responsibility and a willingness to perform what they consider their duty.

They are industrious people who demonstrate pragmatism, an earth quality. Love of detail is often carried to an extreme.

*Understanding Human Nature, p. 14, 286.

Tidiness shows in their activities and practicality hallmarks their attitudes. Their generosity is easily recognized but when it is taken for granted resentment is shown, and if pressed too hard they are able to "refuse" to comply with requests and stand firm in their decisions.

On the negative side of the coin there is too much criticism, and the overly critical attitude becomes an unwanted detriment as a result of discimination carried too far. In the effort to achieve something very practical, the Virgo type may fail and this makes him resentful at his incompetence so that he shows impatience, nervous irritability and bad humor. He can be cantankerous and snap at some pointed remark. He can make mountains out of molehills and display unsuspected temper which is slow to cool.

The Mother instincts, often too forceful in the feminine type, can become so overbearing that it creates a psychological problem for the Virgo child, the object of this exaggerated domination. Thwarted with the denial of his freedom, the young Virgo develops a rebellion which often remains a problem for him later in life.

For the spiritually advanced man, former excessive critical or analytical tendencies are transformed through illumination and the Christ Consciousness is able to shine forth. Virgo illustrates how service of the "immediate present" exemplifies the reaction whereby the God Immanent evokes response from the "form side of life," and in so doing itself is served.

Alice Bailey, writing in *From Intellect to Intuition*, makes clear that "when a man has gained control of the mind and can offer it to the Soul as a transmitting agent, then a vast region of spiritual awareness can unfold itself. The Soul then can become a transmitting agent and pass on via the mind and thence to the physical brain, some of the realizations and concepts of the Spirit aspect."*

Dane Rudhyar enlarges the picture in describing how "growth means transformation or change in conditions. This change requires taking a new step forward, or, if the motion is negative, backward. In every new step a person takes, there is a moment during which he is off balance, having left a previous state of equilibrium (or stability) and not yet having reached the

*From Intellect to Intuition, p. 138.

state ahead. This off-balance state indicates a crisis. All crises are transitions between two states or conditions of existence or consciousness...

"Illness may be the direct result of some defeat of the vital energies unable to cope with a challenge to grow stronger, or an attempt by the soul to impress upon the consciousness the need for a revision of attitude, or the normal sign of bodily disintegration in old age. It may also be imposed upon the body, or the mind by the violent impact of some over-all social crisis, war or revolution...

"One should not forget, however, that for the individual to respond to a social or national need is the normal way to grow; this normal way does not inevitably require that he pass through some acute crisis or experience illness. What is demanded is that he contribute to the productivity and growth of his community, and this contribution usually takes the form of employment or service."*

● ● ●

In summing up, the mission in Virgo shows that it is primarily to nourish the Soul and as the growing awareness of the Higher Self is increased, the desire to service is heightened, accentuating the nature of the Transpersonal Self. With this inner growth nourishing the Christ Consciousness, the outer expression of service takes the form of helping others, of serving humanity in some form.

Saint Paul's statement, "Christ in you the hope of glory,"** holds the key to spiritual unfoldment in this sign.

---

*The Astrological Houses, p. 91.
**Colossians: 1:27.

LIBRA, THE SCALES
September 23 - October 24

In a tiny pool
You could jump over
I saw reflected all the sky

I wondered: How
Should one rightly measure
This lovely water...
By the Earth that holds it:
By the Heaven it holds?

—Solomon De La Selva

A prime requisite for growth in Libra is a sense of proportion that comes through balancing countless pairs of opposites in daily living. This sign of the Scales is hard to understand because it presents the sum total, the synthesis of the aspirant's past qualities and achievements with the pull backward of the see-saw activity of balancing—the urge of the Soul to go forward and upward, the pull backward of old personality habits and desires trying to dominate.

Libra is considered as a time of "interlude," where the tipping of the Scales becomes the testing point whether to focus on the lower self or rely on the Higher Self; to descend deeper into matter following the involutionary path or climb out of the world of form onto the evolutionary road that leads to spiritual unfoldment. It offers the choice between personality desires and Soul aspiration, and is said to be the sign in which the first real vision of the "narrow razor-edged Path of Discipleship appears."

Libra and Gemini contrast two aspects of duality. In Gemini, the effort is to maintain a fluid interplay between the pair of opposites; in Libra, the goal is to maintain a balance between them, which eventually allows the Soul to dominate and make the final decision to tread the Path of Discipleship which the following sign of Scorpio emphasizes.

The activity of the Libran energies makes possible the descent of illumination from the Higher to the Lower Mind, which carries those flashes of the intuition to become the cause of developing true synthesis where the vision is clear. Self-knowledge is increased and there is freedom from fear.*

There is no single point of crisis in Libra since the sign itself is considered to be "an extended crisis" forming a triad of crises with Leo (individuation) and Capricorn (initiation). This critical condition of Libra is a result of the progressive influence of all the other nine signs with the conditions which have arisen from their activity.

The sign of the Scales has a triple expression as:

1. *Law,* demonstrated as legislation, legality and justice (balance).

2. *Sex,* manifested as attraction, union and cohesion.

3. *Money,* understood as concretized energy with its creative potential.

When the power of right choosing has been developed, these aspects are expressed in a positive way, for a certain amount of wisdom relfects that attribute of the Universal Mind—Love which qualifies the manifestation.

Two notes sound forth in the Libran struggle for growth:

The Personality calls out: Let choice be made.

The Soul proclaims: I choose between the two great lines of force.

*Esoteric Astrology, p. 227.

Cosmic Rays and Planetary Rulers

THE RAYS

Three rays control here—the Fifth Ray of Concrete Mind or Science ruled by Venus exoterically, the Seventh Ray of Ceremonial Law and Order ruled by Uranus esoterically, and the Third Ray of Active Intelligence ruled by Saturn hierarchically.

The Fifth Ray of Concrete Mind or Science is the light bearer and responds (in time and space) to the Light of the Logos both (1) as a receiver of illumination when contacts are made or (2) as the illuminator for the lower plane. All energies produce both positive and negative results for the mind is constructive if forwarding spiritual progress, negative and destructive if, blidning true vision, it becomes the "slayer of the real."

The Fifth Ray functions in three ways: as *Abstract Mind,* receiving impressions from the spiritual will; *as the Son of Mind,* expression Soul intuition with spiritual Love-Wisdom; *as the Thought-Form Agent* for the Concrete Mind.

The Seventh Ray of Ceremonial Law and Order deals with the building forces of Nature, relating the form to the life aspect. It is known sometimes as "the ray of executive work" whose purpose is to build, coordinate, and establish cohesion in the four lower kingdoms of nature. It affects individuals, it creates widespread relation between the Soul and the lower concrete mind, marking the first stage of a creative life when they become more closely related and eventually enter into a conscious recognized association on the astral plane.

When a man is treading the Path and is between the first and second initiations, this ray helps him express consciously and increasingly a desire to help his fellow men; and so he establishes a relationship between himself and them. All the time the ray is influencing the individual, it works toward making him grow into the likeness of what he essentially is. Finally, its activity reaches a culmination at the Third Initiation of the Transfiguration.*

Ritual is basic to Seventh Ray operation. That is, ritual understood not in a religious sense but in a wider concept as a method of organization found in the world of commerce, finance or in all great enterprises. *It is a pattern or rhythmic orderliness.*

*The Rays and the Initiations, p. 574-576.

On astral levels its energy restores order within the emotional consciousness.

Coming into power in this antechamber of the Aquarian Age, it first works negatively by making the materially-minded man more selfish and more self-centered, clouding reality with glamour. Positively, it strengthens his capacity to stand steady at the center of his being as he builds constructive throught-forms.

The Third Ray of Active Intelligence. Its qualities will be discussed in detail in the section on Capricorn, where it is exceedingly powerful.

THE PLANETS

Venus. This exoteric ruler of Libra qualifies all it touches with the energy of mind for it is the carrier-agent of the Fifth Ray. Her mission in Libra differs from her functioning in Taurus and Gemini, for here she affects the personality and makes possible the sublimation of passion into love. In the early stages of man's evolution she accentuates his desires, but later she effects the sublimation of passion into love through the channel of aspiration. In the early stages of growth, she also demonstrates embryonic brotherly love.

Uranus, God of the Sky and of the Ether, Uranus appears as ruler first in Leo where he is veiled by the Sun. In Libra, he works esoterically through the Seventh Ray by bringing into materialization whatever is needed to manifest the relation of spirit and matter. However, it must be understood that this "bringing together" is the "relating of physical need and psychical need through the power of creative imagination." It is through Uranus that an intense interplay of the energies of Libra and Aries produce the needed equilibrium for the earlier latent Arian forces.

This planet initiates a new order of conditions and living for the disciple; it reveals underlying causes and brings truth to the surface, and is the urge that heightens the Libran desire to make the change from the old to the new. It is Uranus who fosters spiritual consciousness—the intuition leading to inspiration.

Saturn. The hierarchical ruler of this sign is Saturn, familiarly known as Father Time, the Grim Reaper who will be examined more fully in the section of Carpricorn where his potency is felt both in the field of matter and of spirit.

Self-Actualization and Self-Realization

> Values do not drive a man, they do not *push* him but rather *pull* him...if I say a man is pulled by values, what is implicitly referred to is the fact that there is always freedom involved: the freedom of man to make his choice between accepting or rejecting an offer, i.e., to fulfill a meaning potentiality or else to forfeit it...
>
> I never tire of saying that the only really transitory aspects of life are the potentialities; but the moment they are actualized, they are rendered realities; they are saved and delivered into the past, wherein they are rescued and preserved from transitoriness. For, in the past, nothing is irrecoverably lost but everything irrevocably stored.*

The main problem for the Libran is the constant practice of weighing values, of achieving the right equilibrium between whatever pairs of opposites confront him. He must be able to distinguish between two kinds of equilibrium: a lower, static one qualified by "compromise," and a higher, dynamic type. Solutions for all problems must be made on a plane higher than the originating level. The balance sought for, and the control of the forces are not gained in supressing or neutralizing them but by regulating them for constructive use and purpose.

> The fundamental polarity between the human personality as a whole and the Transpersonal Self can...be resolved into a unity. This is the aim of a long process of transmutation, involving a protracted series of conflicts, approaches, and contacts, each producing a partial or more expanded fusion.
>
> Conscious living can be thought of as a constant polarization and tension between different kinds of tendencies and functions, and continuous perseverance, conscious or not (on the part of the journeyman) to establish equilibrium.**

Equilibrium of diverse kinds, adjustments and integration are produced in many ways. In some instances crises and conflicts

*Man's Search for Meaning, pp. 157-8, 190-1.
**The Balancing and Synthesis of the Opposites, p. 5.

precede them; in others balance is reached by more harmonious methods, and the wing of the pendulum between extremes gradually decreases the oscillations.

The key for adjustment lies in a *lack of identification with either of* the pairs of opposites, but mainly in rising above their level and seeking the solution of the problem there.

• • •

Relating to the physical body, Libra rules the kidneys and the small of the back. In the emotional body it fosters the need for affection and harmony; thereby avoiding discord and conflict. Some astrologers credit the Libran as being of a gracious nature, modest, refined and artistic, adaptable, cheerful, tactful, sympathetic and forgiving. Opposing these characteristics are those of indecision, sitting-on-the-fence, overbalancing, along with uncertainty, aloofness, carelessness, vacillation and even recklessness.

• • •

Writing in *Man's Search for Himself,* Rollo May shows the necessity of "accepting responsibility for one's own standards and judgments, even though one knows how limited and imperfect they are.

"This is what Paul Tillich means by the courage to accept one's finiteness...the acting, loving, thinking, creating the courage to be and trust one's self despite the fact that one knows he does not have the final answers and he may well be wrong. But it is only from a courageous acceptance of 'finitude,' and a responsible acting thereon, that one develops the powers that one does possess—far from absolute though they may be.

"To do this presupposes the many sides of the development of consciousness of self...including self-discipline, *the power to do valuing* (underscoring, ed.)...Obviously this requires a considerable degree of integration, and the courage it requires is the courage of maturity."*

According to the *Secret of the Golden Flower,* "the step to the higher consciousness leads away from shelter and safety. The person must give himself to the new way completely, for it is only by means of his integrity that he can go farther..."**

---

*Man's Search For Himself, p. 238.
**Richard Wilhelm. The Secret of the Golden Flower, p. 93.

The joy of Self-Realization is reached only after great discipline is established, for "he who seeks to obey the impulses of the Soul has to cultivate a truthfulness with himself which is rare...in the private moment of his life and in the secrecy of his own meditation let him not gloss over one fault, not excuse himself along a single line. Let him learn to diagnose his own...deeds, and motives, and to call things by their true names.

"Only thus will he train himself to spiritual discrimination and to learn to recognize the truth in all things by their true names. Only thus will the reality be arrived at and the true Self be known."*

*Alice A. Bailey. *Treatise on White Magic*, p. 585.

SCORPIO, THE SCORPION
October 23 - November 22

Test, trial and triumph are the keynotes of this eighth sign of the zodiac where the control of the personality vehicle is a constant struggle that finally leads to triumph. When this goal is reached, the lowest of its two symbols, the scorpion, has undergone a change and emerges as an eagle symbolizing the conquest of personality weaknesses and the transformation of the lower self into an effective agent for Soul expression.

The strings of life experiences have been endured and the Higher Self has transformed a rebellious personality into a willing agent for its bidding, making the disciple an "eagle" which can soar into the realm of higher evolution.

By sounding their notes the Personality and the Soul reveal their aims: On the side of Matter, the call goes forth: *"Let Maya flourish and deception rule."* On the side of Spirit: *"Warrior I am and from the battle I emerge triumphant."*

Scorpio is the sign of discipleship. It provides "points of crises" and "moments of reorientation" which carry its very specific tests to the physical plane where they must be experienced and dealt with. And after they have been faced squarely and handled successfully at the lower level, the life of the man is carried up into heaven, "lifted into the air," where the problems are solved by the use of the reasoning mind.

This "lifting up into the air" is a symbolic reference to the eighth labor of Hercules. The legendary hero finds that the only way he can destroy the loathsome Hydra of nine self-perpetuating heads is to get down on his knees, raise the monster out of the mud, hold it in the air in the light, where he can slay it. The heads correspond to the nine personality tests which the Scorpio subject has to face and surmount; the *kneeling down* signifies the need for humility.

These nine tests are always self-initiated, not imposed upon the disciple. They concern readiness to undertake disciplines which will make spiritual unfoldment a progressive achievement. The trials reveal for the most part that which has been hidden in man's nature as weakness, and each trial represents a challenge on the physical, emotional and mental levels.

1. *Tests of Appetite:* (physical plane)

Natural tendencies in the animal nature. *Sex* - the relation of the pairs of opposites; these can be selfishly handled or "divinely blended"

Physical comfort - life conditions selfishly used.

Money - concretized energy monopolized for selfish purposes.

2. *Tests of Desire:* (astral plane)

Natural tendencies in the emotional nature where desires produces automatic effects on the physical plane. These are more subtle influences.

Fear - conditioning activities today.

Hate - conditioning relationships.

Ambition - desire for power, conditioning objectives.

3. *Tests of Mind:* (mental plane)

Concerning the lower concrete mind. *Pride* - intellectual satisfaction making the mind a barrier to the Soul.

> *Separativeness* - the attitude of
> isolation making the mind a barrier to
> right group relationships.
>
> *Cruelty* - satisfaction gained with
> the mind used as an instrument of
> power for personality wishes; the
> worst kind of fault is not physical
> in nature but more mental.*

When these tests have been successively passed and the weaknesses sublimated, then the two-fold Scorpio goal is reached —right relationship with the Soul and right relationship with the environment. At present it is said that the masses fall under the influence of Libra; world leaders, disciples, aspirants, and intelligentsia are tested by the energies of Scorpio.

Invariably it is easier to see faults in others than to recognize our own. An anecdote about Plato and Diogenes illustrates this:

> One day when visiting Plato's room, Diogenes became very aware of its luxurious surroundings—shelves with glittering silver goblets, sumptuous furniture and a table covered with a rich cloth. Unable to control his rising disdain, Diogenes grabbed the cloth, threw it on the floor, stamped on it and sneeringly cried out, "I tread on Plato's pride," to which Plato quietly commented, "And with greater pride."

When the "warrior" Scorpio reaches a relatively high stage of spiritual unfoldment, life becomes very difficult for him. He realizes the duality of his nature and is confronted with the battle of the opposites—the Dweller on the Threshold (the sum total of his personality weaknesses) and the Angel of the Presence (the Soul). The struggle is terrific until the lesser light of the little self fades into the Great Radiance of the Higher One.

Esoteric Astrology, p. 203-207.

Cosmic Rays and Planetary Rulers

THE RAYS

Two rays dominate in this Sign of Discipleship—the Sixth and the Fourth.

The Sixth Ray of Discipleship and Idealism with its emotional quality controls both exoterically and esoterically. Scorpio, being a part of the "water" triad with Cancer and Pisces, is involved with regeneration, where Cancer emphasizes generation. In Scorpio it manifests devotion to tread the Path of Discipleship and willingly accepts the demands for attaining spiritual unfoldment.

The Fourth Ray of Harmony through Conflict provides the hierarchical influence by stirring up struggles which cleanse and purify the character to make spiritual growth ongoing.

THE PLANETS

Mars. This God of War sets his seal on trials, tribulations, tests and triumph for the striving disciple. In Aries, his impulse leads to gaining exterior experience; in Scorpio, wielding the Sixth-Ray energies, he acts in double capacity of both exoteric and esoteric ruler, affecting the personality as well as aiding the Soul to evolve with greater vision that liberates and makes service more effective.

Mars is often evaluated only in a negative way with little appreciation of its beneficent influence when its dynamism acts as a purifying factor. In the physical body Mars affects the blood stream and since "the blood is the life," it reaches all the organs.

Pluto. Whereas this planet is not listed as a ruler of Scorpio, Mars is regarded as its alter ego. Lord of the Underworld, Pluto is associated with happenings below the surface and, symbolically speaking, it is constantly digging deep into the form-life to destroy old patterns that new ones may be created. This First Ray activity, which it expresses, paves the way for the Second Ray energy to build new forms in order that the Soul may move forward to more effective spiritual expression. When the disciple is advanced to the initiate state, it destroys the cord that links personality to Soul and frees the Higher Self from bondage to the lower self, thus opening the way for experience on higher planes of evolution.

Only once is Pluto listed as a planetary ruler and that is in the sign of Pisces where it impresses its strength esoterically.

The idea of "death" links Pluto to Scorpio (considered as the sign of Death) but in a reference over and above any physical meaning. Pluto is concerned with destroying weaknesses of the personality, particularly pride, which nourishes separation.

Mercury. Messenger of the Gods governing the human family, Mercury is the hierarchical ruler of Scorpio with the purpose of creating crises that open up new conditions for better understanding of Divinity. It is through the conflict engendered by the Fourth Ray energy carried by this planet that the disciple or initiate begins to recognize the Unreal from the Real.

Scorpio is a "water" sign, part of the triad which includes Cancer and Pisces. Concerning the physical body it governs the sex organs, the procreative and regenerative processes and the blood.

Self-Actualization and Self-Realization

Actually, in real life, the Scorpio's struggle-to-be is a long uphill climb to new levels of integration and is not an automatic process of re-education. It involves an expansion of consciousness which will bring new insights, the making of conscious decisions, and a willingness to endure the possible pain and suffering of adversity that come when the disciple has to move forward into new mansions of the Soul.

The transformation of the excesses of the lower self into attributes of the Transpersonal Self demands the use of spiritual imagination and the changing of personality desire into Soul aspiration.

Opposition does not stop the dedicated man from "climbing," for like the serpent he needs rough ground in order to make headway. Obstacles are the very means by which he moves upward for they are truly stepping stones to his goal. Any mountain climber will tell you that if the way is smooth it is bound to be slippery, and with no foot-holds to use in lifting there is a lack of means for ascent.

Climbing to new heights of understanding demands a kind of honesty with oneself which is hard to achieve. It requires that truthfulness with no excuses be given and it is stated that: "...in the private moments of a (man's) life and in the secrecy of his own meditations let him call things by their true names.... Only in this way will he train himself in spiritual discrimination and learn to recognize truth in all things. Only thus will reality be arrived at and the true Self be known."*

Scorpio is a sign of extremes. Its lower type shows a personality of a very materialistic nature where emotions run rampant at times and sensuality and passion dominate. On mental levels, the individual is capable of intense mental cruelty, especially sarcasm—the sting of the scorpion's tail. Self-mastery is the essential mission for him. The Scorpion with the sting in its tail must be left behind if the eagle is to fly high and become aware of new concepts of truth that will make possible future expressions of a high spiritual quality and the victory of the Higher Self.

Offsetting the negative qualities of Scorpion bluntness, tyranny and vindictiveness are the admirable traits of fearlessness, optimism, devotion, patience, abundant vitality, a positive attitude and the ability to penetrate "with the eagle's eye."

At times the Scorpio nature manifests as being overly critical not only of itself but of others as well. This is illustrated in showing attachments to both the "good" and the "bad," where devotion is seen as following some worthy ideal or selfish ambition. Occasionally, clinging to possessions or ideals shows a kind of loyalty that does not easily forgive or forget.

In offering a method of handling the problem of drives, emotions and desires, Dr. Roberto Assagioli explains that the solution lies not in suppressing them or in condemning them on their own account, but in using the *skillful will*. This means refraining from giving them any interest or attention and employing the even more powerful technique of *substitution*— concentrating on the antithesis of bad qualities, replacing them with good ones, such as courage for fear, joy for depression, moderation for greed. This creates *neutralization* and tends to give immunity to negative harmful influences.

*A Treatise on White Magic, p. 585.

An old adage states that "the Will of God drives the world, but the Love of God determines the result." If the disciple can continuously manifest Love, Self-Realization will bring the necessary control of weaknesses and faults of the personality, and then the Soul can affirm: *"Warrior I am and from the battle I emerge triumphant."*

SAGITTARIUS, THE ARCHER
November 21 — December 22

To have a goal in life is to be blessed for it provides a sense of direction which makes the ongoing toward the objective one-pointed.

"Every time a man finds himself under the influence of Sagittarius, the third of the fiery signs,* it is with the objective of orienting himself to some new and higher goal with the unfoldment of some basic directing purpose.

"These developing purposes range all the way from purely animal desires...to the liberation toward which the entire evolutionary process has impelled him."**

In this ninth sign of the zodiac, the path leads from ambition to aspiration, from selfishness to an intense desire for selflessness, from individual one-pointed self-interest (Leo) to the one-pointed preparation for initiation in Capricorn.

Motivation is the prime factor for this sign of the Archer whose three symbols trace the Sagittarian picture:

First, there is the Centaur, halfhorse, halfman, who aims his arrows toward the gratification of animal desires; this is *duality expressed by man and beast attached.*

*The fiery trilogy consists of Aries, Leo and Sagittarius.
**Esoteric Astrology.

Second, the archer *on the horse; man and beast separated, duality unattached;* now the arrow is aimed toward self-development.

Third, finally, the arrow is alone with a bit of the bow across its shaft; direction finally points toward illumination of the mind through the agency of the Soul. *Freedom from attachment.*

This symbol of the horse has prevailed throughout the ages, being popular in the time of Atlantis and mentioned in the ancient Vedic hymns of India. Not only do we find references to it in the East, but also in the West as in these Biblical verses:

And I saw, and behold a white horse; and he that sat upon him had a bow... (Revelations 6:2)

And I saw heaven opened, and behold a white horse; and he that sat upon him was called Faithful and True... (Ibid 19:11)

And the armies that were in heaven followed him upon white horses... (Ibid 19:14)

Classified as a human sign, Sagittarius is deeply concerned with the intuition illustrated by the familiar story, that should a man's aspiration reach a great height it will touch the field of Buddhi, of wisdom; and the arrow that the archer let fly as aspiration will return to him as the arrow of the intuition. Direction for this shooting is said to be a beam of light whose strong focus reveals a still greater light that in turn illumines the way to his goal. For vision ever leads the dedicated server to his ideal.

In the beginning the personality sounds this note: *Let food be sought.*

But once the disciple begins to serve his fellow men, the Soul sounds it clarion call: *I see the goal, I reach the goal and then I see another.*

In order to discover where the arrow of the intuition has led him, the Archer has to dismount from his horse (symbolically). When he does this and discovers the location of his goal, he realizes that at last he can travel on "the wings of the Soul."

In ancient archives it is recorded that it was Sagittarian energy that enable the Christ to foresee His great sacrifice. Echoes of this are written in the Bible: "He steadfastly set His face to go to Jerusalem" (Luke 9:51).

In the growth of man's consciousness there are three important signposts that mark its evolution:

Instinct governing desire, mass consciousness characteristic of the sign, Cancer.

Intellect governing ambition, individual consciousness, Leo.

Intuition govening aspiration, early manifestation of *Soul consciousness, Sagittarius.*

The process involving the transmutation from one state of consciousness to another is a very slow one. The instinctual life of the unevolved man in Cancer falls below the threshold of consciousness when the intellect of Leo takes over; in turn, the intellect is superseded by the intuition when the Soul sheds its light of illumination. By this time the emotional nature is under control, and the reasoning power of the mind is called into action by the Soul whose quality, infused into the personality, dispels glamour and releases the man from illusion: "He is inspired from on high."

Cosmic Rays and Planetary Rulers

Rays Two, Three and Six press their influence in Sagittarius bringing Love-Wisdom, Active Intelligence and Devotion and Idealism.

Jupiter. King of the Gods, Jupiter is the exoteric ruler channeling Second Ray energy characterizing his out going quality and expansiveness. This planet, the largest of the satellites, is the only agent besides the Sun which carries the Second Ray of Love-Wisdom, the basic ray of our solar system.

As a viceroy, Jupiter dispenses his power as a ruler showing an inclusive nature which can be generous (typical of the Jupiterian "expansiveness"), very warm, optimistic and jolly (jovial). Sympathy, loyalty and faithfulness add to his virtues. But these positive traits can be suppressed by a display of impatience, irritation, a lack of temperance (again, over-expansiveness) and a resulting extravagance. On occasion, his imperious nature shows a lack of love intelligently applied while injustice and hypocrisy dominate his actions.

The Earth. Our globe transmits the Third Ray of Active Intelligence, and as the esoteric ruler of Sagittarius it promotes Soul unfoldment. Mentality, as its title suggests, is a foremost characteristic, and this it fosters so that the Soul may more easily send its messages to the brain.

For the developed man, it constantly nourishes a sense of inquiry. Also in the background is that earthly trait of practicality, which keeps the feet on the ground when the ideas of the Sagittarian tend to fly off in many directions into the wild-blue yonder of the "abstract" and fail to hold to the line of needed one-pointedness. At this stage the blend of the Second and Third Rays provides the restraint for balanced judgment, and extremes are avoided.

Mars. The hierarchical ruler, with its Sixth-Ray drive, has to cope mainly with keeping "devotion" oriented to high ideals.

Self-Actualization and Self-Realization

The main problem for the Sagittarian is reorientation and direction.

In this ninth sign of the zodiac, Self-Actualization demands discipline of fiery personality traits, for this sign of the Archer is the third in the fire-triplicity of Aries (spiritual fire), Leo (solar fire), and itself fire by friction—Spirit, Soul and Body.

In relation to the physical body, Sagittarius rules the thighs and the large muscles that make physical travel easy. The man born under its influence loves the open spaces; he needs to feel free whether he is traveling physically or mentally.

Where creativity is concerned on the physical level—procreation—it must be transmuted into an expression of a higher plane.

Vitaltiy is generously supplies for this lover of the outdoors, of sports and exercise in general. While travel on a physical level attracts him, so does exploring on the mental plane where new ideas challenge his curiosity with excitement. He is fortunate in that his inquiring mind, sometimes too trustful, and his spontaneity are checked by a sense of "earthiness" which keeps him from being an impractical idealist. However, he must be watchful and not let a tendency to exuberant enthusiasm override a sense of proportion.

Ralph Waldo Emerson once said that nothing was ever achieved without enthusiasm. On the other hand, Dag Hammarskjold sees it from another angle:

> I am being driven forward
> Into an unknown land.
> The pass grows steeper,
> The air colder and sharper.
> A wind from my unknown goal
> Stirs the strings
> Of expectation.
>
> Still the question:
> Shall I ever get there?
> There where life resounds,
> A clear pure note
> In the silence.*

There may be doubts for the Sagittarian but these are fleeting, for his vision carries him forward to his goal. And although he may have doubts about the "reason" for some activity, when it comes to the "ongoing" he is no laggard. He pursues his ideal with a confidence supplied by his native intuition, and is steadfast in his striving guided by the inner perception of the Soul.

By listening to the Voice of the Silence, he learns the value of when to be silent, to tune down his self-assertiveness, moderate the desire to be individualistic, temper self-centeredness and be willing to listen to the other point of view. What he acutely needs is to develop tolerance. He has to curb bluntness which is expressed without restraint and know that one cannot always speak the truth forcibly for then it can hurt, not heal. Restraint on many levels must be cultivated, for the expression of freedom must be wisely handled.

Gordon Allport, in his book, *Becoming,* enlarges the concept of freedom by saying:

Markings, p. 5.

To choose one's attitude in a given set of circumstances ...is the ultimate freedom recognized by the ancient Stoics as well as by modern existentialists...intentional characteristics represent above all else the individual's primary modes of addressing himself to the future. As such they select stimuli, guide inhibitions and choices, and have much to do with the process of adult becoming...philosophically speaking, values are the termini of our intentions....*

● ● ●

The Archer is forever shooting his arrows into the "unknown." These keywords mark his evolutionary growth: *Let food be sought.* (personality centeredness) *I see the goal, I reach the goal, and then I see another.* (Soul centeredness)

"Without the dynamism of his motives," states Roberto Assagioli, "no matter how clear his aims or worthwhile they may be, a person can lack the drive to go on and remain only a dreamer instead of the doer of willed action."**

According to the esoteric teaching of the Ageless Wisdom, reorientation comes with the finding of some new goal. The direction leads higher and higher to the world of Spirit. One-pointedness keeps the Sagittarian on the Path, and the more evolved he becomes the more joyous is the pursuit of his arrows of aspiration.

Man's search for meaning is a primary force in his life and not a "secondary rationalization" of instinctual drives. This meaning is unique and specific in that it must and can be fulfilled by him alone; only then does it achieve a significance that will satisfy his own will to meaning...man...is able to live and even die for the sake of his ideals and values!...***

*Becoming, p. xiii, 89 and 90.
**The Act of Will, p. 150.
***Man's Search for Meaning, p. 154-155.

CAPRICORN, THE GOAT
December 22 — January 20

Of all the signs, Capricorn, the tenth, is said to be the most mysterious. According to the Wisdom Teaching, its graphic symbol is intentionally made undecipherable and sometimes is referred to as "the signature of God." It has never been correctly drawn.

"I am the densest point of all the concrete world. I am a tomb; I also am the womb. I am the rock which sinks itself into the deep of matter. I am the mountaintop on which the Son is born, on which the Sun is seen and that which catches the first rays of light."*

As an earth sign, Capricorn expresses "the densest point of concrete materialization of which the human soul is capable. Man is the 'of the earth, earthy'...'the first Adam.' In this sense, Capricorn holds in itself the seeds of death and finality—the death which takes place finally and eventually in Pisces... When crystallization has reached a certain degree of density and so-called 'hardness,' it is easily shattered and destroyed and man, born in Capricorn, then brings about his own destruction; this is due to his fundamentally materialistic nature, plus the 'blows of fate' which are the enactments of the law of karma. Again and again, a certain measure of concreteness is achieved, only again to

*Esoteric Astrology, page 432.

undergo destruction, prior to the release of the life and the rebuilding of the form."*

Whether as an individual or as an initiate going through the strenuous tests of advanced discipleship, the Capricornian must sustain great effort to meet the strain and struggle that confront him and be conquered on the physical plane.

Three animal symbols reveal much about his nature. First there is:

The Goat: an earthy animal representing the greedy, selfish human being goaded by desire to satisfy the desires of his senses; he scavenges among the rocks symbolizing the physical plane environment.

The Crocodile: living on land and water relates to the emotional aspect and because of this duality, consciousness in the early stages of development is a blend of the animal nature (earth) and desire (water). Even in later progress there can still remain some residual weakness which, despite any high motivations in general, shows self-centeredness on the astral plane.

The Unicorn: pictured in white (purity), is the fabulous creature whose horn reaches out from the center of its forehead. This signifies the triumphant disciple, the Initiate, The Christ or Soul—*The Unicorn of God, the Omnipotent.***

Capricorn is the *birthplace of the Christ consciousness* and is the fourth in a series. Aries marks the first in the pattern of development, with subjective activity producing the urge for the Soul to incarnate or perhaps to have some Hierarchical Plan come into being. Cancer is the second, the entrance into the life of physical form—dense physical matter—bringing *instinctual mass consciousness.* Leo is the third, individuation, the realization of *self-awareness, self-assertion, individual consciousness.* Capricorn, climaxes with *spiritual consciousness,* being "born again" into life in the Higher Worlds after taking the first of the major cosmic initiations, the Transfiguration, which gives the Initiate his first glimpse into the nature of the Will of God.

To reach the stage of transfiguration, the Capricornian will have surmounted three tests:

1. *Experience of Depth in the Valleys,* faced in Scorpio where the intellect is heightened by the inflow of the light of the Soul;

*Esoteric Astrology, p. 158.
**Esoteric Astrology.

2. *Experience of the Plains,* endured in Sagittarius, the testing ground that demands holding steady on the narrow Path, falling neither back into the valley nor to the side of the road losing direction. Always the objective is seen clear—casting aside, overcoming all personality attachments in order to proceed onward and to the far-ahead goal, the mountain top.

3. *Experience on the Mountain Top,* where the "seeker" climbing on his knees has to learn humility (symbolically) is sustained in his trial by the support of the "intuitive flashes" which are produced by the Soul as it irradiates the personality with its quality to process fusion. After reaching the summit of the mountain, the Initiate, having become illumined during this final test, has a freedom of personality to choose future areas for incarnation.He may choose to enter life-in-form through the Gate of Cancer to serve the Masses, or select Capricorn to fulfill some specific world need as a World Initiate.*

Keywords describe progress on the evolutionary path with the personality sounding its note: *Let ambition rule and let the door stand wide;* and with the Soul letting its note ring clear: *Lost am I in Light supernal and yet on that Light I turn my back.*

And so "the old Soul takes to the road again," now to perform as a World Initiate prior to becoming a World *Server* in Aquarius and finally a World *Server* in Pisces.

Cosmic Rays and Planetary Rulers

THE RAYS

Two Rays are influential in Capricorn, the Third and the Fifth.

The Third Ray of Active Intelligence. "I am the worker and the Work" pictures the expression of this energy which is the ray of the human kingdom. It is concerned with form and the physical body, and involves evolution.

Our Planetary Logos is a Third Ray Ruler and at this moment in time, expressing Himself through our earth globe, using it to manifest Spirit as He takes a cosmic initiation.

Spirit is Matter at its highest and Matter is Spirit at its lowest.

The "active intelligence" of the Third Ray is demonstrated by its power of discrimination in its mental activity. The activity

Esoteric Astrology.

counterbalances the note of Love which is the basic and dominant note of our solar system and the cause of our evolutionary development. "Life enters the forms, thanks to this discriminating and selective activity, and passes from one experience to another in a wider scale of contacts."

This innate intelligence was developed in the previous solar system (the first in a series of three). It is potentially found in the substance used in our current solar system because in the earlier period, Matter was impregnated with the quality of Mind. That which evolved through experiences (the result of this union) became our instincts which now have fallen below the threshold of consciousness. In view of this conditioning, we recognize the substance forming the bases of current multitudinous forms is not "virgin soil."

Modern science attests to the occult interpretation of this powerful intelligent matter in its recognition of the astounding performance of the DNA molecule. J. Brownowski, in his revealing book, *"The Ascent of Man,"* describes the functioning of its double helix:

> The DNA spiral is not a monument...it is...a living mobile to tell the cell how to carry out the processes of life step by step. Life follows a time-table, and the treads of the DNA spiral encode and signal the sequence in which the time-table must go.*

The Third Ray of Active Intelligence is classified as a Ray of Aspect in the cosmic trilogy, with the First Ray of Will or Power and the Second, of Love-Wisdom. This Third Ray, sometimes called the Ray of Adaptability, has four subsidiary *Rays of Attribute:* the Fourth Ray of Harmony through Conflict, the Fifth of Concrete Mind or Science, the Sixth of Devotion and Idealism and the Seventh of Ceremonial Ritual and Law and Order—all of which are synthesized by the Third Ray.

The Fifth Ray of Concrete Mind or Science governs the entire Fifth Plane, and in humanity it stimulates the will-to-manifest through the activity of the "fire of Mind." In Capricorn, it is effective when the disciple is well advanced in spiritual unfoldment. Here its hierarchical influence produces a higher form of

*The Ascent of Man, p. 395.

love revealed as compassion and loving understanding, which bespeaks of its close relation to the Second Ray of Love-Wisdom.

THE PLANETS

Saturn carrying the Third Ray plays a double role acting as both exoteric and esoteric ruler in this sign of the Goat. As one of the Four Lords of Karma, Saturn is a forceful taskmaster and makes a man face his mistakes and weaknesses of the past and present as it prepares him for the future.

Familiarly know as Father Time, Saturn is often mistaken as being a malevolent factor in his activity of creating negative conditions. However, to the contrary, he is in reality a benevolent force; he produces unwanted opportunities that test man's potentials and reveal shortcomings that must be overcome for spiritual development. These "trying" conditions are truly stepping stones to greater maturity.

Venus. Along with the Fifth Ray hierarchical ruler of Capricorn, Venus (formerly acting exoterically in Taurus and Libra and esoterically in Gemini) brings in energy from a source outside the solar system with the purpose of aiding the Higher Self to complete its fusion with the personality. As stated earlier, Venus is the alter ego of the Earth and their close rapport began in time immemorial when animal man became *homo sapiens.* Their relationship is mutually beneficial.

● ● ●

The great task, the supreme test for the Capricornian, is to reach the mountain top where he becomes transfigured—an experience clearly defined in two examples: Moses receiving the Ten Commandments on Mount Sinai and Christ receiving illumination on the Mount of Transfiguration.

In the Old Testament, the giving of the Law expresses the activity of Saturn using the Third Ray and commanding obedience to Divine Wishes. In the New Testament, it is Venus who sheds the beauty of Spirit demonstrated by the Christ as the embodiment of Love and mind, preparing for His initiating the New Era of the Brotherhood of Man.

Capricorn guards the secret of the Soul itself and reveals it to the Initiate at the time of the Third Initiation, which is sometimes called the "secret of the hidden glory."

Self-Actualization and Self-Realization

> Courage is the basic virtue for everyone as long as he continues to grow, to move ahead...as an inward quality (it is) a way of relating to one's self and one's possibilities...as this courage in dealing with one's self is achieved, one can with much greater equanimity meet the threats of the external situations...
>
> It takes courage not only to assert one's self but to give one's self...as the inner side of growth (it is) a constructive way of that becoming of one's self which is prior to the power to give one's self.*

With earthiness as an inherent characteristic, practicality is strongly marked in the Capricornian nature. Down-to-earth makes demands that Self-Actualization and Self-Realization be resolved on the physical level where the aspirant must get down on his knees (the part of the body ruled by Capricorn) to learn the needed humility for climbing to his goal.

The Capricornian is industrious; he can also be patient and persistent, showing his endurance to maintain when challenges occur. A tendency to be conservative appears in his desire to cling to the past; he is apt to be expedient at times with a materialistic attitude far from admirable. There is a certain confidence in his own rightness which must eventually be eliminated if he is to identify with the Soul; he must let go of fixed ideas if he is to reach Self-Realizaiton.

Ambition lies deep within him and is a major problem when it comes to conquering some negative aspect of its drive. Gratification of the senses can also be troublesome, and desire for spiritual awareness must be sublimated into a different kind of aspiration. Nobility of motive may not change the nature of a selfish ambition, for to be truly rewarding selfishness has to be transmuted into a form of unselfishness.

Some astrologers give the Capricornians a quality of independence, a love of justice and self-reliance; they enjoy controlling not only their own affairs but also those of others. And, where money is concerned, it is merely a means to an end.

*Man's Search for Himself, p. 224-225.

Transcendence and elevation demand stern discipline. The final struggle for ascension is exceedingly difficult because it means not only raising the consciousness but raising it above all that is material. The central test in Capricorn is to free onself from past habits and personal hindrances—the experiences and achievements one clings to. "It is the battleground of the old established order and habits and the higher inclinations and tendencies."*

In Capricorn, the conflict exists between its earthy or stabilized aspects and its dynamic influence of the urge to move ahead into the future. What the Capricornian needs is not the sporadic flight to higher spiritual levels but a gradual climbing and steady prolongation of the consciousness upon the successive levels reached. In esoteric terms this is seen as the battle between the Dweller-on-the-Threshold and the Angel-of-the-Presence. Victory comes when the Soul, having subjugated the Personality, allows the Initiate to reach the summit of the mountain where transfiguration occurs. There illuminated, he stands in spiritual being sufficiently elevated to receive the great light of the Spirit and to be given a glimpse of the nature of the Will of God.

It is not only the conquest of form that occupies an extremely important and central position in later development under this sign, but also the use of form to express the desire of the Soul as it, in turn, reveals the Will of the Logos. In each sign the Initiate has to express the consummation and spiritual fruit of earlier life experiences, world experiments, and of Soul achievement. The pattern is always the same, requiring selfishness to be transmuted into selfless service and desire into purity of spiritual aspiration to accord with the Will of God.

"Capricorn stands for the influence which will carry the will of Shamballa to the Hierarchy or to the world initiates, giving to Them that dynamic and enterprising spirit which will enable Them to carry forward to completion the Will of God on Earth. It was the 'angel, born under Capricorn' which came to the Christ in the garden of Gethsemane and fused His individual will into the Divine Will and thus enabled Him to carry out His mission to completion. This was not only the revelation of divine love to the world but—as the legend in the Masters' Archives goes on—He

*Esoteric Astrology, p. 170.

came 'to fabricate the gossamer thread which bound the two together and linked the place of the Most High (Shamballa) with the Holy City (The Hierarchy). The bridge between the Holy Place and the Holy of Holies was securely anchored. The Will of god could now be carried to fruition' ".*

To reach the Mountain Top is to gain some understanding of the significance of the energy of Life. For those who have yet to arrive at this High Point there remains much speculation about its nature. But for Albert Schweitzer there was a definite knowing of its omniscience. His well-known statement testifies to this:

> Reverence for life means to be in the grasp of the infinite, inexplicable, forward-urging Will in which all Being is grounded. It rises above all knowledge of things. It leads to a union with the ultimate reality which is "the infinite Being in infinite manifestation."**

*Esoteric Astrology, p. 632-3.
**Social Philosophies of an Age of Crisis, p. 181.

AQUARIUS,
THE WATER CARRIER
January 21 - February 19

So much has been written about Aquarius as the harbinger of the New Age that there is no need to emphasize its importance as the beginning of a new era or of its promise to usher in the eventual "life more abundantly."

Aquarius is pre-eminently a sign of constant movement and of changing conditions. For those who realize this and are willing to adjust to its demands, prepare for them, accept them and put them into use, it offers the opportunity to achieve:

Brotherhood - Unity - Synthesis - World Service.

This eleventh sign of the zodiac is classified as an "air" sign and it demonstrates pervasiveness, rapidity, mutability and subtlety.

When a man keeps going deeper and deeper into "form" on his evolutionary journey, he becomes more and more blinded by illusion and increasingly materialistic, which dominates his personality. The note he sounds as he continues to gratify his senses is: *Let desire in form be ruler.*

Despite the fact that he may be group minded (an outstanding characteristic of the Aquarian nature), in the early stages of his development he subverts its constructive potential for humanitarian purposes and uses the "group" to further his selfish personality aims or ambitions. Eventually self-centeredness is sublimated into aspiration to help others and the former materialistic aspect of his nature is "dissolved into air." Group-mindedness becomes a sustained attitude to offer help where it is needed, and all the while the consciousness continues to develop a sense of group responsibility. When this takes place the Soul proclaims: "Water of Life, I am poured forth for thirsty men."

This "water" is symbolized by two pictures: one, the astrological glyph of two wavy parallel lines and the other the drawing of a man carrying a pitcher on his shoulder from which flows the stream of life-giving energy. In the Last Supper, Christ sent his disciple into the city to find a man bearing a pitcher of water on his shoulder. Twice He spoke of the power of water: "He that believeth in Me shall never thirst," and again, "If any man thirst let him come unto Me and drink." (John 6:35, 37).

• • •

Universality is a recurrent theme in Aquarius, emphasizing spirit as the universal water-of-life. Along with it is the awareness of the imporance of the "group" in the life experience. As this awareness grows, so grows the realization that individual relationships are secondary to those of the group.

Three keynotes of this sign are easy to understand in theory but difficult to demonstrate in practical living for the tasks are arduous.

First, the disciple must transmute service for the little self into that for humanity.

Second, he must change superficial selfish activity into selfless effort to aid the Hierarchy in implementing the Plan.

Third, he must accomplish the transition from self-conscious living into "sensitive humanitarian awareness."*

When these transformations are taking place there still remain traces of individuality expression. When the man experiences spiritual unfoldment, he becomes more conscious of the fact that he is no longer an isolated unit separated from humanity but a definite part of the Whole. And, although he retains his identity he sees it in a different perspective, recognizing it as relative to the *larger evolutionary pattern of living usefulness*.

*Esoteric Astrology, p.

As is to be expected, depths of depression and heights of ecstacy round out the ongoing experience but periodically the depression is lessened. As it begins to fade, the light of the Soul—which has been continually poured into the personality—produces a heightened sense of spiritual power.

Cosmic Rays and Planetary Rulers

THE RAYS

Rays Seven, Two and Four cast their power in this sign of the Water Carrier; they are felt more at the beginning and at the end of the life journey than during the middle of it. As with all cosmic energies it is their combined influence that produces a synthetic effect on the individual Aquarian.

The Seventh Ray of Ceremonial Law and Organization predominates at present. Just as the Sixth Ray of Devotion and Idealism typified the Piscean Age, so the Seventh Ray highlights the Aquarian. "Not often in the great cosmic cycle does one ray follow another in numerical sequence and when this does happen there eventuates a rapid following of effect upon cause and this today can provide the basis for assured hope."*

The Seventh Ray is sometimes known as the *Ray of Magical Order.* In carrying out its purpose of creating relationships, it strongly reflects that aspect of the First Ray of Will and Power by demonstrating the will-to-relate which expresses the act of will that relates spirit and matter.

Since this Seventh Ray is the most influential energy of the New Age, those born under the eleventh sign of the zodiac will be open to its concentrated impact. Whether or not they react to it depends on their sensitivity at the individual point in evolution.

No one can evade ritual or ceremony. It is everywhere around us although it is common not to recognize its expression: the rising and the setting of the sun, the ritual of the passing years; even breathing illustrates a constant rhythm (ritual). Ritual may be seen in the individual or in the great activity of Deity carrying out a universal pattern.

*A Treatise on the Seven Rays, Volume I, p. 358.

THE PLANETS

Uranus, Jupiter and the Moon are the powers that leave their mark on the "Water Carrier."

Uranus. The domain of this God of the Sky is the "ether." The environmental characteristic of ether is pervasiveness that penetrates not only the entire region of outer space but "interpenetrates matter and all bodies existing in it."

As the exoteric ruler of Aquarius, Uranus conditions personality growth distinguished by the quality of speed and disruptive change. However, we are told that its forceful purpose is to better life conditions, and in bringing a continuous urge for change Uranus drives humanity to seek the "new." Although not immediately recognized as such, Uranus is working toward a brighter future as it creates opportunities for expanding consciousness with new patterns in livingness and a new order of society.

Since Uranus is identified with the "ether" it is natural that it should also be identified with the "etheric body," both human and cosmic. In the human body it affects the calves of the legs and the ankles. It constantly stimulates the urge to explore, particularly to adventure into the unknown. This accounts for it being the planet of occultism, seeking hidden causes of outer effects.

This volatile satellite of the Sun is laying the foundation for the New Age, giving promise of the eventual establishment of the Fifth Kingdom of Souls on the physical plane.

Jupiter. The largest of the planets, Jupiter is the esoteric ruler of this sign and carries the energies of the Second Ray of Love-Wisdom as it aids Uranus in unifying Spirit and Matter. Here is exemplified the Jupiterian quality of expansiveness working on Soul level as it expresses inclusiveness, moving toward synthesis and the resolution of a greater Whole.

Both of these planets in their effective cooperation contribute to "the ultimate glory of the Solar Logos" using Humanity as a focal point to distribute their energies for the individual man.

The Moon is the hierarchical ruler and, carrying the energy of the *Fourth Ray of Harmony through Conflict,* affects the advanced disciple in such a way as to direct his activity toward creating World Service.

The number "four" has particular relation to our earth which is being used by the Planetary Logos to express Himself in physical form.

The Earth is: *the fourth Globe*—one in a series contained in *the fourth Chain*—part of a series of seven Chains which is used by the Planetary Logos as means for gaining cosmic initiation.

The Earth is: *in the fourth Round*—a path of Time in the journey of the Logos taking His cosmic Initiation; *receiving the Fourth Ray* influence from the Moon which creates the condition of a crucible for the initiate or disciple to distill harmony from conflict and thus establish an environment where humanitarian activities can prosper.

Self Actualization and Self Realization

If there were a question to describe Aquarius in a few words, two can be chosen for the answer: *Group and Service*. As stated earlier, the self-centered, selfish Aquarian uses the Group to serve himself, the unselfish one serves the Group. Extend this latter idea and you reach Brotherhood; extend it cosmically and you embrace Universality.

"The most important sphere of giving," says Erich Fromm, "is not that of material things, but lies in the specifically human realm. What does one person give to another? He gives of himself, of the most precious thing that he has, he gives of his life.

"This does not necessarily mean that he sacrifices his life for the other—but that he gives him of that which is alive in him; he gives him of his joy, of his interest, of his understanding, of his knowledge, of his humour, of his sadness—of all expressions and manifestations of that which is alive in him. In thus giving of his life, he enriches the other person, he enhances the other's sense of aliveness by enhancing his own sense of aliveness.

"He does not give in order to receive; giving is in itself exquisite joy; but in giving he cannot help bringing something to life in the other person and this which is brought to life reflects back to him, he cannot help receiving that which is given back to him. Giving implies to make the other person a giver also and they both share in the joy of what they have brought to life. In the act of giving something is born, and both persons involved are grateful for the life that is born for both of them. Specifically with regard to love this means: love is a power which produces love..."*

An Aquarian described by astrologer Llewellyn George is one having a faculty of discrimination with a quiet, patient, unobtrusive manner; he is friendly, generous, charitable as he displays his humanitarianism... As a lone wolf he can be very detached in his feelings for the individual as he is more concerned for humanity itself. He does not care for many persons save a few including his family and some close friends. The spiritually undeveloped Aquarian usually has only a superficial caring for the group and this must be translated into genuine feelings at a time when the Soul is released from its prison in matter and can express its own characterisitic of group-mindedness. Faith and loyalty exist as personality traits but when a man is on the Path these have to be superseded by dedicated service for group benefit.**

Not to be overlooked is the quick temper displayed by the Aquarian at times but he does not hold resentment. However, he will not be driven for he loves freedom (Uranus). He can be thoughtful and at times both philosophical and intuitive and often radical in attitude.

The effectivness of Ray influence shows in the drive of the Seventh toward external organization in all fields of life, a tendency toward standardization and even regimentation. The Second Ray produces the magnetic forces drawing toward comradeship and friendship, a result of spiritual urging with this orientation eventually leading to sharing with large groups and working toward world unity.

At all times moderation is the keynote for a balanced life. Here in Aquarius the problem lies between emphasis on the individual and collective consciousness, with the *noble middle path* achieved through applying a mediating principle to group consciousness and group life.

Since the Seventh Ray is of such strong influence in this sign the disciple is constantly aware of being pressed towards the goal of relating Spirit to Matter. Resolving the pair of opposites into a *functioning Whole on the physical plane* is a major problem for Self-Realization. This awareness can make the Aquarian more

*The Art of Loving, p. 24-25.
**A to Z Horoscope Maker and Delineator, p. 243.

extroverted than introverted. In order to reach the desired equilibrium, he must avoid the extreme of self-depreciation as well as the exaltation of heightened spiritual power. It becomes obvious that over-extroversion grows into exhibitionism and the ecstatic feelings of intensified spirituality into spiritual pride. The problem is resolved by keeping the consciousness so rooted, so centered at Soul level that the Higher Self makes possible the balance of an alternation in right proportion, which is in reality harmony emerging from conquered conflict (Fourth Ray).

The advanced Aquarian disciple or Initiate, having achieved a high degree of balance, can pour water from his pitcher in a deliberate and controlled way—so regulated that it never becomes empty because he is constantly refilling it, drawing from the pool of spiritual life, the Soul, ever giving forth *the Water of Life.*

> All energy is born of relationship. It is produced or released by the interaction of currents of desire or of compassion flowing from the polarities of the universal Whole, as well as from those within human bodies or personalities. Energy is relationship in act. It is the productive "fact" of relationship. Man's attitude towards this fact—the use he makes of it—establishes the character and quality of his participation in society and in the universe...*

Triptych, p. 175.

PISCES, THE TWO FISHES
February 20 — March 20

Pisces is a sign of extremes. During the early cycles of growth, the Soul's experience is deeply imprisoned in matter. The captivity is pictured by the Piscean symbol of two fishes, Body and Soul, held together by a band—the Sutratma of Eastern philosophy, the Silver Cord in the Bible. During man's aeonic journey in evolution, the cord is gradually loosened by the Soul's influence on the personality until the tie is finally broken and the Soul is free to return to its source, the Father's House—Spirit.

Three stages show this development:

1. Bondage or captivity.
2. Renunciation or detachment.
3. Sacrifice and death.

The goal of Pisces is saviourship with the objective to save through sacrifice—large or small. "...The fusion or blending of soul and form as far as man is concerned, produces the manifestation of the Incarnated Christ, the perfected individual soul, the completed manifestation of the microcosm. Thus the greater and the lesser polar opposites—the human being and God, the microcosm and the Macrocosm—are brought to their destined expression and manifestation...

"The goal of Deity, and the emergence of God's plan and the nature of His eternal purpose is for us only a subject of interested speculation. There is a possibility that this plan and purpose may be vastly different to our surmise which is based upon our formulation of a Deity who is the product of our mental processes and of devoted idealism (two of the three aspects of the personality nature), and the attempt to interpret His infinite purposes in terms of our own finiteness."*

Pisces, one of the "water" signs in the triad of Cancer and Scorpio, displays a fluid temperament in the early periods of growth when it is open to all types of contact due to its high sensitivity and mediumistic quality. The consciousness is instinctual and long stretches of time pass before this stage is transmuted into the intellectual which in turn leads to further spiritual development. Meanwhile, the germ of the Christ life lies dormant for the mind is not sufficiently developed to register subtle impressions to awaken it. It remains a latent potential; "the hidden Christ is unable to free itself from contact with the water."

As long as personality is in control, the hidden power of the Higher Self remains negative. This causes Pisces to be regarded as a sign of "inhibition and hindrances" where the animal and personality powers—particularly the emotional—predominate in the undeveloped type of Piscean. But once the mind is stabilized by the mental activity of the polar opposite sign of Virgo, then its critical and discerning faculties allow the intuition to register impressions on it. These are low impressions made over a period of inordinate time until the transmuting and transforming processes result in changing servitude into service and the man is able to rightly evaluate "Truth."

The interpretation of the intuition in the Wisdom Teaching is very different from its ordinary conception as being "hunches" or indescribable ideas. The esoteric viewpoint considers it to be an attribute of the Soul, an expression of Wisdom over and above the reach of the Abstract Mind which carries its messages and acts as an agent for its reflection. Psychiatrist Roberto Assagioli assesses it to be "a higher form of vision etymologically related to vision and means to see within—'in-tueri'—at its highest it can be equated with a directional suprarational, comprehension of the nature of reality..."**

Sensitivity is an outstanding characteristic of Pisces and it is

*Esoteric Astrology, p. 115.
**The Act of Will, p. 225.

displayed in the duality of psychic attributes—Lower and Higher—Mediumship and Mediatorship. Mediumship is manifested in low-grade psychism, mediatorship in the highest, and is exemplified in the perfected Christ. Mediumship is expressed in mass consciousness; impressionable, sensitive and receptive. In contrast, mediatorship reflects the Christ consciousness, group consciousness, universal consciousness; its energy is that of the Buddhic, intuitional control of the low psychic nature.

Higher psychism used by humanitarians or disciples promotes discrimination which will evoke the "will within themselves." This puts them in touch with the will aspect of Deity which is the Will of God stepped down from Shamballa to Hierarchy and finally to Humanity. Eventually man himself becomes a radiation of spiritual will that affects humaity.

The victory at the end of the Path in Pisces is the result of the tests endured by the personality where the "little will," carried up into the realm of the Divine Will, evokes inspiration and the emergence of a World Savior—"Not my will but Thine be done."

Thus it is seen that this is an aspect of will-energy working out as the will-to-save. It is powerfully implemented by the activity of the Second Ray underlying our entire solar system, producing the Christ consciousness, the Self-Realization that objectifies the Christ principle.

Cosmic Rays and Planetary Rulers

THE RAYS

Only two rays dominate in Pisces—the Second Ray of Love-Wisdom influencing the personality and the First Ray of Will or Power working to benefit the Soul.

The Second Ray shows its effect in the early stages of growth when it tightens the cord between the personality and Soul. This is a necessary activity during the early stages of evolution when its cohesive power strengthens the needed bond between the two.

The First Ray with its destroying power illustrates how the death of form makes possible the release of the Soul from its mortal coil, giving it the freedom to return to its source, the high realm of Spirit. The triple aspect of this will-energy throws much light on the variety of its functioning in several signs:

Taurus: Vulcan ruling—demonstrates the will-to-know, the will-to-illumine.

Virgo: The Moon veiling Vulcan—provides the urge of the will-to-be-in-form, the urge of the Soul for "Beingness."

Pisces: Pluto—furnishes the will-to-save.

Two keywords reveal a clear picture of the Piscean pattern: For the personality: And the Word said: Go forth into Matter. For the Soul: I leave the Father's Home and turning back I save.

THE PLANETS

Jupiter, the exoteric ruler of Pisces, maintains the Soul's early imprisonment in form by holding the cord secure with the power of the Second Ray. This "binding" is essential to give time for the creation of a multitude of experiences that will condition the personality to become an affective instrument for spiritual expression. There is no escape from this pattern until such time when the Soul has infused its quality into its instrument to such a degree that the cord is ready to be cut and the final relationship to the past destroyed.

It is said that "in every human being, head and heart, mind and love, will and wisdom express a duality. It is the work of Jupiter to develop these qualities and bring them into a synthetic interplay."*

Pluto. Only once is this King of the Underworld, the legendary brother of Jupiter, listed as a planetary ruler and it is in this twelfth sign where he effects death and destruction of old patterns by digging deep into dark, hidden places. Pluto cleans out whatever debris is blocking the path of the Soul for spiritual expression. It never destroys the consciousness aspect but destroys the wrong kind of desire and other hindrances that obstruct the way to liberation for the Higher Self. After resurrections have been made and many transmutations and transformations accomplished, the Transpersonal Self is then able to ascend to greater height and move into new cycles of adventure in the world of Higher Evolution. At present, Pluto only evokes response from those disciples and groups who are sufficiently evolved to respond.

Esoteric Astrology, p. 126.

"Pisces governs the feet, hence the whole thought of progress, of attaining the goal, and of treading the Path of Return has been the underlying revelation of the Great Cycle through which we are now passing..."*

Self-Actualization and Self-Realization

In discussing the desire for Self-Realization in his book, *Foundations for a Science of Personality*, Andras Angyal evalutates life as a "tendency to shape one's life course into a meaningful whole which gives coherence and unity to the life history."** He adds to this idea by saying that "the intrinsic purpose in the life of the person...is definitely connected with a feeling of responsibility... Life is regarded as a unique opportunity and it is felt to be a duty to shape the life course into something worthwhile..."***

Dr. Angyal sees the personality structure as being built along three main dimensions: those of progression, depth and breath. He enlarges the meaning of progression by describing it as a "structure of means-end relations that is being built" and goes on to explain that "a clearly defined and fully accepted purpose brings a definite concentration into the person's activity, and thus the means-end structure, being firmly organized, increases the energy output, the efficiency, and the productivity of the person."†

In speaking of the dimension of depth in its greater development he sees that it is "an increased metaphysical anchoring of one's personality, the formation of a philosophy of life and a system of values giving a more or less clearly defined meaning to one's life...

"To grow in the dimension of *breadth* (transverse dimension) means to open up more channels for the expression of one's behavior tendencies... The fullness of life depends upon a harmonious growth of the personality structure in all three dimensions."‡

Esoteric Astrology, p. 128-29.
**Foundations for a Science of Personality*, p. 355.
***Ibid.*, p. 354.
†*Ibid.*, p. 356.
‡*Ibid.*, p. 357.

According to Clark E. Moustakas, "the self is not in its definition or description but rather the central being of the individual person. The self is not definable in words. Any verbal analysis tends to categorize or segment the self into communicable aspects or parts. The self can only be experienced. Any attempt to convey its meaning verbally must be based on function or structure and on language which can be partially understood. Therefore comparison, relatedness, and association to situations and events are required in a communicable definition of self. When the self is understood only in words the experience of the self is lost. The self as experienced involves the totality of the individual. It is a natural, automatic and complete expression, only partially available to verbal communication. Understanding of self is possible through unqualified perception and empathy, that is, human presence and being."*

● ● ●

The main problem for the Piscean is knowing how to handle sensitiveness. And in regard to any recognition of psychism in his nature, he must strive to transmute clairvoyance into spiritual perception of vision and change any presence of clairaudience into telepathy of high quality.

Biblical parables often contain hidden significance in their surface meaning. One of these is Jonah and the Whale where Jonah's rebellion and final recognition of Divine Intent relates symbolically to the Piscean struggle between the Lower and the Higher Self and final victory for the Spirit. "The parable is concerned with the Piscean stage of consciousness and the awakening of the Christ consciousness with the consequent dispute which that entails. Jonah stands for the hidden imprisoned Christ, alive to the perils of the situation, and the whale of large size stands for the bondage of incarnation and for the personality."**

Astrologer Florence Jensen depicts Pisceans with a discerning eye when she points out that they are "agreeable, acceptable and versatile, but they lack will-power and dynamism. They can be very determined on the outside but underneath they tend to bog down when the going is difficult. They must learn to take a stand.

*The Self, p. 11, 12.
**Esoteric Astrology, p. 123.

Pisces' element is water which flows smoothly when life is calm but Pisceans will churn and make waves when they cannot have their own way...and will stir up a hurricane when anything or anyone makes them unhappy... Calmness should be cultivated ...but when Pisceans have a fixed goal nothing will stop them. They have strong underlying traits."*

Alan Leo enlarges this portrait by describing a Piscean which he says is "capable of lifting himself by his own bootstraps... impressionable, romantic, imaginative...flexible with a restless mind always searching for new ideas; tormented with curious fantasies he (the Piscean) is easily moved by proximity with others...

"His mind is...just, kind, benevolent and powerful... Generous, he commands a poetical contemplative spirit, he is studious and likes to enjoy himself; though changeful he can develop a strong will and exercises authority without harshness, being firm in a pleasant way.

"He is prudent but does not readily bind himself; slow to anger, critical though without prejudice, hard to appease, yet often content with a noble vengeance; he undertakes too many pursuits; passions are strong but changeful and any wealth acquired is the result of his own efforts and works."**

For the Piscean to achieve his goal he must fulfill several demands:

1. He must create a synthesis embodying balance and equilibrium attained only when the negative characteristics have been overcome.
2. He needs to develop a discriminating mind supplemented by an enduring will; he must minimize hypersensitivity of emotional attachments; negative conditions must be absorbed; all must be necessary for spiritual unfoldment made possible by the mind which changes former fluidity into current balanced control.
3. He has to merge the personal will with the "all-embracing Divine Will" demonstrating "the will that Loves and the Love that Wills." These achievements will enable him to stand in spiritual being—to *live at the Center.*

*Horoscope Magazine, March 1974, p. 101.
**Astrology for All, p. 183.

For Abraham Maslow, "Psychological health is indicated by appreciating that a human being has within a pressure (among other pressures) towards unity of personality, towards full individuality and identity, towards seeing truth rather than being blind, towards being creative, towards being good and a lot else.

"That is, the human being is so constructed that he presses towards fuller and fuller being and this means pressing towards what most people call good values, towards serenity, kindness, courage, knowledge, honesty, love, unselfishness and goodness."*

Erich Fromm echoes the basic teaching of the Ageless Wisdom when he declares that "There is only one passion which satisfies man's need to unite with himself, with the world and to acquire at the same time a sense of integrity. This is *love*...it is an experience of sharing, of communion, which permits the full unfolding of one's own inner activity."**

And so at the end of his spiritual journey the Piscean, having attained full Self-Realization, expresses the Christ-like qualities which are indentified with the Transpersonal Self. His intention to achieve has been supported by his will-to-achieve. He has affirmed the power of his will and so expresses the characteristic of the "light" of Pisces:

"The Light of the World revealing the Light of Life Itself."

* "Psychological Data and Value Theory" in: New Knowledge in Human Values, p. 126.
**"Values, Psychology, and Human Existence" in: New Knowledge in Human Values, p. 152-53.

POLARITY

For the person seeking Self-Actualization and Self-Realization, an important key to understanding the influences of the energies of the signs lies in knowing the relationship of the pairs of opposites which constitute the signs' polarities. This relationship is a determining factor in the expansion of consciousness.

In the context of this primer, polarity constitutes an alignment between two signs 180 degrees apart from each other, making six pairs of opposites out of the twelve signs: Aries-Libra, Taurus-Scopio, Gemini-Sagittarius, Cancer-Capricorn, Leo-Aquarius, Virgo-Pisces. The interplay of their energies produces mutual benefit on a spiral path of experience, first in one and then in the other, gradually affecting a synthesis of the two which blends into the power of the Whole.

Djwhal Khul, in teaching the Ancient Wisdom, postulates that in reality there are not twelve zodiacal signs but only six, for each opposite acts as a complement for its other half. The dynamic interplay of their forces works toward a singleness, a unity arrived at as a result of the activity of one sign unfolding in spiral progression to develop a greater consciousness in the other.

● ● ●

From a psychological point of view, Roberto Assagioli points out that "fundamental polarity between the human personality as a whole and the Transpersonal Self can be resolved into a unity.

"This is the aim of a long process of transmutation involving crises, a protracted series of conflicts, approaches and contacts, each producing a partial or more expanded fusion... This constitutes the highest effort, the central aim of the man who consciously or unconsciously aspires to this goal or is pushed towards it by his inability to find lasting satisfaction or true peace until he has attained it.

"Various equilibrations, adjustments and integrations can be produced in different ways," says Dr. Assagioli. "In a number of cases they are preceded by intense crises and conflicts. At other times they are reached in a more harmonious way be means of a gradual decrease in the oscillations of the 'pendulum' which swings between the extremes...

"The essential requirement is to control, transmute and direct the energies of the opposites from a higher unifying center of awareness and power. This involves the use of 'wisdom,' an attribute of which is playing with the opposites to regualte the antipodal forces and functions and thereby establishing a dynamic equilibrium and synthesis without resorting to compromise, but rather by regulation from a higher level."*

ARIES-LIBRA (Fire-Air)

The first pair of opposites on the zodiacal wheel is Aries-Libra. Here the activity of spiritual energy demonstrates in Aries as the will-to-create and then in Libra as the will-to-balance. This will-to-create works toward the will-to-good that is accomplished in Libra where the will appears as the will-to-express proportion and harmony of Soul and Personality—a synthesis which is brought into existence through sublimation, a transmutation which changes the lower condition into the higher one through the constant influence of the Libran power to balance.

If, when reaching Libra, the "seeker" has found no fulfillment to gratify his personality desires, he then begins to change his life style and turn away from his habitual pursuit of satisfying the senses and look inward for some answer to his problem. For many incarnations there is a working toward humanitarian service until finally a certain amount of stabilization is established, on returning to Aries on a higher turn of the spiral, the initiate reaches the

*"The Balancing and Synthesis of the Opposites." p. 7-9.

end of his journey in the world of form (in Pisces). Upon reincarnating in Aries he moves to that realm of Higher Evolution to progress further toward spiritual evolvement.

TAURUS-SCORPIO (Earth-Water)

The second pair of opposites, Taurus-Scorpio, presents a focus on desire which must be transmuted from its lower expression on personality levels to aspiration on the higher plane of Soul. Desire-Aspiration-Direction (Will) correspond in wide perspective to man-the-personality, man-the-Soul, man-the-channel-for-Spirit. The lower desires of the early Taurean period are intensified when the individual seeking personal gratification reaches Scorpio. It is not until he has decided to tread the Path and undergo the nine tests which Scorpio requires for personality transmutation that aspiration begins to dominate his nature. The spiritual imagination can then dispel and begin to dissipate the glamour of the unreal world. The self-indulgence initiated in Taurus is overcome in Scorpio and the selfless attitude of the disciple prevails. Ambition is replaced by "the executive activity of the Soul," and former personality desires become transmuted into the "tenacity of Soul purpose."

Earth and Water (Taurus and Scorpio) must be blended and related, and it is this truth connected with these two signs which lies behind all teaching on baptism and purification. "The earthly material desires of Taurus must in due time be brought under the influence of the purifying water in Scorpio."

Baptism by water (a name for the Second Initiation) needs a preparatory period of testing and purification, and this the Scorpio experience is intended to give. After the Third Initiation (the Transfiguration) when the Soul is released from personality control, the testing power of Scorpio is no longer felt and the darkness of the experience in this eighth sign of the zodiac becomes illumination in Taurus on a higher turn of the spiral.*

GEMINI-SAGITTARIUS (Air-Fire)

The third pair of opposites is the second combination of Air and Fire, the first being Libra-Aries. The keynote here is a question of direction, the outstanding characteristic of their relation. In

*Esoteric Astrology.

Gemini, the direction is "to" and "fro," personality to Soul and vice-versa; in Sagittarius, the direction is one-pointed, Soul-ward.

The fluidity of Gemini is seen in two stages: first, as the will-to-be in form; second, as the will-to-be-free from form. The last stage indicates the control of the Soul over its personality which is expression in a fusion of the two and is known as "fluid-synthesis."

Gemini presents many struggles between Soul and personality; Sagittarius reveals the contest between the Higher and the Lower Mind aiming at Soul control with an unswerving drive toward Higher Consciousness. At the beginning the Sagittarian one-pointedness is directed toward Soul level. The early indecisiveness (characteristic of the Sign of the Twins), is eventually supplanted and transformed into a sustained effort of the Soul in preparing for initiation. Finally, when the Initiate returns to Gemini, he is receptive to its highest aspect of consciousness of Love-Wisdom, the basic energy of our Solar System.

CANCER-CAPRICORN (Water-Earth)

These two gates of birth signify the fourth pair of opposites. Cancer, the first gate into incarnation, opens to the life in form and mass consciousness; Capricorn, the second, relates to opening into the life of Spirit when the disciple has achieved the third or the *first major cosmic* initiation, the Transfiguration. Here he gains his first knowledge of the nature of Spirit. Life in form should never be underestimated. It is a component part of the life cycle on Earth. To repeat, without form and without the ability to bear in mind the need to respond sensitively to the environing conditions and circumstances in the three worlds, the Soul would never awaken to knowledge and therefore never know God in manifestion. The building of adequate forms and the control of form are essential if there is to be wise and right cooperation with the Plan of God.

The whole story of the Soul's progress through matter and the release from it can be seen in the use of the mind in the conflict and the life in form. The release from it obviously comes from the control and the right use of mind which illumines and brings strength gained through the tests in Scopio in advance of the subsequent trials in Capricorn. Time and time again rebirth occurs in Cancer to continue the on-going life pattern in form until after aeons there comes the urge to climb the "mountain of Capricorn" and to discover the life of Spirit. After the third, the first major cosmic initiation, the Initiate by his own will decides which gate he will enter—Cancer perhaps, with the purpose of using *form* to serve the Masses, or Capricorn, to help solve some pressing world problem. Capricorn touches rock bottom in materialism. But having once climbed out of its depths and reaching the heights of advanced spirituality, world service becomes a joyous service.

It should be kept in mind that life-in-form is a necessary experience in the long journey of evolution, and that Cancer accentuates the "matter" aspect whether it is the masses influencing and dominating man's mind or man serving the masses in a humanitarian way. In the Cancer-Capricorn experience, the consummation to be achieved is the transmutation of the mass consciousness (in Cancer) into the Christ or Soul consciousness (in Capricorn), a necessary bridge leading to the group consciousness of Soul consciousness. In Capricorn, Transpersonal Consciousness becomes the hallmark of the World Initiate.

LEO-AQUARIUS (Fire-Air)

All signs emphasize the development of consciousness to a degree, but for Leo, the Lion of Self-Assertion (fire) and Aquarius, the Water-Carrier of life-giving spirit (air), consciousness becomes a keynote in this fifth pair of opposites.

The aggressive individualist, Leo finds after many lives that self-centeredness does not bring fulfillment of a longing which the many experiments of gratifying his senses have failed to produce. Satiety has shown him it is not the means he needs. He looks for a direction to follow and eventually orients his aspiration to a higher level where, discovering group consciousness, he touches his inner, real Self. And in so doing he comes into contact with the reflection of the positive aspect of his polar opposite, Aquarius.

Struggling on the Path of Discipleship, the neophyte begins to realize that he must sublimate his personality yearnings and transform them into expressing right human relations, the goal of which is the ideal of brotherhood. This demands a point of view that is universal, always working for the greatest good for the greatest number. This is the "synthesis" characteristic of Aquarius and indicates Unity and Wholeness, always an endeavour *pro publico bono.*

Not to be overlooked is the potential of the Leo individual to rise to heights of the polar opposite expressing the best kind of leadership, the beneficence of kingly guidance where strength serves the multitudes. One need not be a king to demonstrate this benevolence, for long before he has reached the state of a World Server, he can be a blessing to mankind by displaying the high aspect of the Leo nature—unselfishness.

Thinking only in terms of the positive aspects of the Aquarian is to lack understanding of the whole of his nature. In the early stages of his evolvement, he exhibits a selfishness in using the "group" for his own benefit, a tool to work for his own advantage. It is only when he is dedicating his services to his fellow men that the noble aspect of Aquarius is revealed in his livingness.

VIRGO-PISCES (Earth-Water)

The last and sixth pair of the polarities completes the pattern of fusion in consciousness which gives a picture of the six "wholes." Once their complementary nature is recognized, the blended relationship indicates its potency in offering "the freedom of the two," for the apparent twelve signs are known to be in reality only six.

In this combination of Virgo-Pisces, there is a working out of synthesis where the early dominant fluidity of Pisces is stabilized by the mental control of Virgo so that the Christ Consciousness, which is hidden in the beginning, is given a chance to grow in the womb of Virgo, the Virgin. There in darkness, instinct is transmuted into intellect and experiences in depth bring one crisis after another to prepare the way for the Soul to move out of the dark into the light during the long period of the gestation of consciousness.

It is the mind developed by Virgo that brings about the needed transmutaton, with the Soul becoming more and more conscious of its control over its vehicle. This activity develops the faculty of analysis and criticism and changes the psychic fluid Piscean quality into that which reveals the illumination and intuition latent and dormant from the very beginning of the incarnation. In the final achievement, the "macrocosm" and the "microcosm" meet, the greater and the lesser, Deity and the human being. When this happens, the Soul moves on to greater achievements of Spirit.

WHOLENESS:
THE IDEAL DIMENSION

Self-Actualization and Self-Realization
work toward making a man
Whole.

"The factor or principle called 'holism' underlies the synthetic tendency in the universe, and is the principle which makes for the origin and progress of wholes in the universe....

"This whole-making or holistic tendency is fundamental in nature, that it has a well-marked ascertainable character, and that Evolution is nothing but the gradual development and stratification of a progressive series of wholes, stretching from the inorganic beginnings to the highest levels of spiritual creations ....

"Holism is matter and energy at one stage; it is organism and life at another stage; and it is mind and Personality.... All its protean forms can in a measure be explained in terms of its fundamental character and activities...."*

It is true I must begin with myself but I must never be an end in myself.

—Lao Tzu

*Holism and Evolution, Preface v and p. 320.

What we call the beginning is often the end,
and to make an end is to make a beginning.

—T.S. Eliot

"The tendency of the person to make of his life course a coherent, meaningful whole is experienced as a desire for self-realization.... The holistic development may be traced in three basic dimensions of the person: progression, depth and breadth....

"In the dimension of progression, a means-end organization of widening scope may be built. Developments in the dimension of depth creates, on the one hand, deeper metaphysical anchoring of the person's life, and on the other hand, a perfection in expressing one's deeper tendencies in actual behavior. Finally, development in the dimension of breadth means the opening of manifold channels of behavior and a good coordination of the various channels."*

● ● ●

"Love makes the world go round."

"Love is a life-giving force necessary for physical, mental and moral health...

"It is an indispensable condition for deep and lasting happiness.

"It is goodness and freedom at their loftiest.

"It is the finest and most powerful educational force for the enoblement of humanity.

"The extensity of love ranges from the zero point of love of oneself only, up to the love of all mankind, all living creatures, and the whole universe. Between these minimal and maximal degrees lies a vast scale of extensities.... The maximal point of intensity is the love of the whole universe (and of God).... The zero point....is love of oneself only...

"Love beautifies our life because the love experience is beautiful in its very nature and beautifies the whole universe.... Anything that one looks at through loving eyes becomes 'lovely,' that is beautiful...

"Love experience means freedom at its loftiest.... To love anything is to act freely, without compulsion or coercion.... To

Foundations for a Science of Personality, pp. 372-373.

be free means to do what one loves to do.... In this sense, love and true freedom are synonymous.... The love experience is equivalent to the highest peace of mind and happiness.... When it is unbounded and pure, it is 'the peace of God which passeth all understanding...'"*

"You are a child of the universe, no less than the trees and the stars; you have a right to be here. And whether or not it is clear to you, no doubt the universe is unfolding as it should."**

*The Ways and Power of Love, p. vii, viii, 11, 12, 13, 16.
**Found in Old Saint Paul's Church, Baltimore, Maryland, dated 1692.

BIBLIOGRAPHY

ADLER, Alfred, *Understanding Human Nature*, NY: Greenberg Publishers Inc., 1927.

ALLPORT, Gordon W., *Becoming*, New Haven, Conn.: Yale University Press, 1955.

_____ , *The Individual and His Religion*, NY: The Macmillan Co., 1960.

ANGYAL, Andras, M.D., Ph.D., *Foundations for a Science of Personality*, Cambridge, Mass: Commonwealth Fund, Harvard University Press, 1958.

ASSAGIOLI, Roberto, M.D., *The Act of Will*, NY: The Viking Press, 1973.

_____ , "The Balancing and Synthesis of the Opposites," NY: Psychosynthesis Research Foundation, Issue #29, 1972. (pamphlet)

BAILEY, Alice A., *Esoteric Astrology (A Treatise on the Seven Rays III)*, NY: Lucis Publishing Company, 1951; London, Lucis Press Ltd.

_____ , *Esoteric Healing (A Treatise on the Seven Rays IV)*, NY: Lucis Publishing Company, 1953; London, Lucis Press Ltd.

_____ , *Esoteric Psychology I (A Treatise on the Seven Rays I)*, NY: Lucis Publishing Company, 1936; London, Lucis Press Ltd.

_____ , *Esoteric Psychology II (A Treatise on the Seven Rays II)*, NY: Lucis Publishing Company, 1942; London, Lucis Press Ltd.

_____ , *From Intellect to Intuition.* NY: Lucis Publishing Company, 1932.

_____ , *Initiation, Human and Solar,* NY; Lucis Publishing Company, 1951.

_____ , *The Rays and the Initiations (A Treatise on the Seven Rays V),* NY: Lucis Publishing Company, 1960; London, Lucis Press Ltd.

_____ , *A Treatise on White Magic,* Lucis Publishing Company, 1951; London, Lucis Press Ltd.

BRONOWSKI, Jacob, *The Ascent of Man,* Boston, Mass: Little, Brown and Co., 1973.

FRANKL, Viktor E., *Man's Search for Meaning (An Introduction to Logotherapy),* NY: Washington Square Press, 1967, paperback edition.

FROMM, Erich, *The Art of Loving,* NY: Harper and Row, 1956.

GEORGE, Llewellyn, *A to Z Horoscope Maker and Delineator,* Los Angeles, CA: Llewellyn Publications, revised and enlarged eighth edition, 1943.

GREEN, Elmar, "The Menninger Foundation Paper," Council Grove, Kansas: 1969.

HAMMARSKJOLD, Dag, *Markings,* NY: Alfred A. Knopf, Inc., 1977.

JENSEN, Florence, HOROSCOPE Magazine NY: Dell Publishing Co., *(Children of Gemini),* June 1973.

_____ , HOROSCOPE Magazine NY: Dell Publishing Co., *(Children of Pisces),* March 1974.

JUNG, Carl G., *The Integration of the Personality,* London: Routledge and Kegan Paul, Ltd., 1940.

_____ , *The Undiscovered Self,* Boston: Little Brown and Co., 1957-8.

LAO TZU, *The Way of Life,* England: Quotation printed by the Group for Creative Meditation, Tunbridge Wells, Kent.

LEO, Alan, *Astrology for All,* Second edition, London: Women's Printing Society Ltd., 1904.

MAETERLINCK, Maurice, *Wisdom and Destiny* NY: Dodd Mead & Co., 1912.

MASLOW, Abraham H., *New Knowledge and Human Values,* NY: Harper Brothers Co., 1959.

_____ , *Religions, Values and Peak Experiences,* Columbus, Ohio: Ohio State University Press, 1964.

_____ , *Towards a Psychology of Being*, NY: D. Van Nostrand Co., Second Edition, 1968.

MAY, Rollo, *Man's Search for Himself*, NY: W. W. Norton and Co., Inc., 1953.

_____ , *Love and Will*, NY: W. W. Norton and Co., Inc., 1969.

MOUSTAKAS, Clark E., ed., *The Self*, NY: Harper and Brothers, 1956.

OVERSTREET, Harry and Overstreet, Bonaro, *The Mind Goes Forth*, NY: W. W. Norton and Co., Inc., 1956.

RUDHYAR, Dane, *The Astrological Houses*, NY: Doubleday and Co., Inc., 1972, paperback edition.

_____ , *Triptych* ("Gifts of the Spirit," "The Way Through," "The Illumined Road"), Katwijk, Netherlands: Service BV, 1968.

SMUTS, General the Right Honorable J.C., *Holism and Evolution*, NY: The Macmillan Co., 1926.

SOROKIN, Pitirim, *Social Philosophies of an Age of Crisis*, Boston, Mass: The Beacon Press, 1950.

_____ , *The Ways and Power of Love*, Boston, Mass: The Beacon Press, 1954.

TEILHARD DE CHARDIN, Pierre, *The Future of Man*, NY: Harper and Row Publishers, Inc., 1964.

WILHELM, Richard, and JUNG, Carl G., *The Secret of the Golden Flower*, NY: Harcourt, Brace and Co., 1935.